THE EDICTS OF ASOKA

THE EDICTS OF ASOKA

ED. IN ENGLISH WITH AN INTRODUCTION AND COMMENTARY BY VINCENT A. SMITH

ASOKA, KING OF MAGADHA

GYAN

Published by

Gyan Publishing House
5, Ansari Road
Daryaganj, New Delhi-110002
Phone: 011-47034999, 9811692060
E-mail: books@gyanbooks.com

Distribution Network
gyanbooks.com
India, USA, Canada, UK, Australia

ISBN: 978-93-7133-151-7 (PB)

First Published, 1909

2nd Impression 2025

Printed at: Gyan Press, Delhi.

THE EDICTS OF ASOKA
Author: ASOKA, KING OF MAGADHA

CAPITAL OF ASOKA COLUMN AT SĀRNĀTH

THE EDICTS OF ASOKA

EDITED IN ENGLISH, WITH AN INTRODUCTION AND COMMENTARY, BY VINCENT A. SMITH, M.A.

PREFACE.

THIS volume has been prepared at the request of Dr. Ananda K. Coomaraswamy in order to provide lovers of dainty books, who do not care for antiquarian and philological lore, with a readable and accurate version of Asoka's unique sermons and other records in an attractive form.

The gems truly are worthy of the best possible setting.

Since the publication seven years ago of the first edition of my little book in the Rulers of India series entitled "Asoka, the Buddhist Emperor of India" (Oxford, at the Clarendon Press, 1901), the study of Asoka's history and inscriptions has made such advances that many serious changes in the translation have become necessary. The versions now offered, which are published in this limited edition with the consent of the Delegates of the Clarendon Press, are the result of careful renewed study of the texts and all explanatory matter accessible to me. The discovery of the Sārnāth Edict in 1905 has made an important addition to knowledge.

I am indebted to Mr. F. W. Thomas for much valuable assistance, especially in the interpretation of the Minor Rock and Minor Pillar Edicts.

The comment is restricted to the amount absolutely necessary to make the translations fully intelligible to the unlearned reader, and detailed references to authorities are rarely given. I have made a special effort to use the various documents each as a commentary on the others, and to bring out clearly the purport of the teaching given to his people by Asoka as the prophet of *Dharma*, the Law of Piety, in the Buddhist sense.

I am fully convinced, in agreement with M. Senart and Mr. F. W. Thomas, that all the Edicts from beginning to end are distinctly Buddhist, and that the only non-Buddhist records of the reign are the Cave Dedications.

CONTENTS.

INTRODUCTION.

ABOUT the time (October, 325 B.C.) when Alexander the Great withdrew from India, or soon afterwards, not later than 321 B.C., an upstart named Chandragupta Maurya seized the throne of Magadha (S. Bihār), the premier kingdom of Upper India, and quickly made himself master of the whole country to the north of the Narbadā, possibly extending his conquests as far as northern Mysore, which certainly was subject to his grandson Asoka. We know that the bitterly-repented conquest of Kalinga on the eastern coast in or about 261 B.C. was not followed by any other act of aggression committed during Asoka's long subsequent reign of nearly thirty years, and the inference is almost unavoidable that the southern extension of the empire must have been the work of either his father or his grandfather. But it is just possible that Asoka during the unrecorded years from 273 to 261 B.C. may have enlarged his borders by wars which aroused no feelings of remorse in his heart.

Chandragupta, whose usurpation had been planned and effected by an astute Brahman minister, variously named Chāṇakya, Kauṭalya, or Vishṇugupta, the reputed author of a notable book on the theory and practice of government, reigned with great power and might for twenty-four years. He was the contemporary of Seleucus Nicator, one of Alexander's generals, who was crowned king at Babylon in 312 B.C., and is known to history as king of Syria, although he was in reality the lord of Western Asia, Syria forming but a small part of his vast dominion. About 306 B.C. this powerful monarch essayed to imitate the exploits of Alexander, and measured his strength against Chandragupta. No detailed account of the conflict has been preserved, but the briefly recorded result is sufficient to prove that the Indian king repelled the invasion with success, obtaining the cession of the valuable provinces between the Indus and the Hindu Kush in exchange for five hundred elephants, obviously far inferior in value. The rivals came to terms, cementing their alliance by matrimonial bonds, and Seleucus appointed an ambassador to the court of Chandragupta, who, no doubt, sent an envoy on his part, but of that mission no record has survived.

Megasthenes, the ambassador of the Syrian king, fortunately employed his leisure in composing a careful account of India, its government, people and products, so far as he could ascertain the facts. His book has perished, but the pith of it has been preserved in extracts, which suffice to enable the modern reader to realize in considerable detail the social and political state of India at the close of the fourth and during the third century B.C. Indeed, until the way to India was again opened by the Portuguese navigators at the close of the fifteenth century, Europe derived its slight knowledge of the country chiefly from Megasthenes.

We are fairly entitled to assume that the system of government established by the genius of Chandragupta, the first emperor of India, and Chāṇakya, his capable minister, continued unchanged in its essential features throughout the reigns of Chandragupta's son, Bindusāra, and grandson, Asoka. The changes made by Asoka, as far as they are recorded, did not affect the framework of government, being designed solely to promote the growth of conformity with *dharma*, the Law of Piety, or moral rule of life in the Buddhist sense as understood by him.

Assuming the continuity of the political organization throughout the reigns of the three great sovereigns of the Maurya dynasty during a period of about ninety years (*circa* 322 to 232 B.C.), it will be found that a knowledge of Chandragupta's system of government as described by the Greek authors and in the book attributed to Chāṇakya will greatly help the reader in understanding the Edicts and other records of Asoka.

The government was an absolute monarchy, a pure despotism in which the royal authority was supreme and unchecked, resting upon a huge standing army which was paid by the Crown, equipped from the royal arsenals, and well organized under the administration of six Boards. This force comprised 600,000 infantry, 30,000 cavalry, 9,000 war elephants attended by 36,000 men, and many thousands of chariots. When we realize the fact that Asoka enjoyed the full control of an instrument so powerful, and possibly stronger in his time than in that of his grandfather, it is easy to understand his ability to effect the conquest of Kalinga, as described in Rock Edict XIII., and to appreciate the appropriateness of the lofty, imperial tone which he adopts in all his commands. He felt no hesitation in sending his emissaries to distant countries of Asia, Africa, and Europe, in intimating his will to numerous nations on the frontier of his empire, and in imposing upon all his subjects a strict moral code, which interfered with many cherished usages. He could not have done these things if he had not possessed the powerful military weapon forged by his grandfather. One of the six Boards charged with the administration of the armed forces of the Crown controlled Admiralty affairs, and when we remember Asoka's relations with Ceylon and even more distant powers, we may credit him with a sea-going fleet as well as an army.

The empire governed by the Maurya kings was of enormous extent. There is no reason to suppose that the provinces beyond the Indus ceded by Seleucus to Chandragupta were abandoned by either Bindusāra or Asoka, and we know from the distribution of the inscriptions that Asoka held the whole of India from the Himālaya to North latitude 14°, that is to say, nearly as far as Madras. The southern extremity of the peninsula was governed by independent Dravidian powers—the Chola, Keralaputra, Satiyaputra, and Pāndya kingdoms enumerated in Rock Edicts II. and XIII. Ceylon also was independent, but received emissaries from the Indian monarch.

This gigantic empire was administered through the agency of Viceroys, generally members of the imperial family, and an organized bureaucracy. The Edicts refer to four of the Viceroys, as the Princes of Taxila, Ujjain, Tosali, and Suvarṇagiri. On the face of the document—the Brahmagiri edition of Minor Rock Edict I.—which mentions the Prince of Suvarṇagiri, he would seem to have been the Viceroy of the South. Another interpretation which has been suggested is not, I think, tenable. Tosali was situated somewhere in Kalinga on the coast of the Bay of Bengal, and its Prince must have been the Viceroy of the East. Bengal may have been included in his jurisdiction, or may have formed a separate government which does not happen to have been mentioned. The Prince of Taxila naturally would have been the Governor of the North-West, including Kashmīr, and there may or may not have been a separate Viceroy for the trans-Indus countries. Some day, perhaps, the Asoka monuments which doubtless exist in those regions will be found. The Prince of Ujjain in Mālwā must have been the Viceroy of the West. According to literary tradition Asoka before his accession served his apprenticeship in the art of government as Viceroy of both Taxila and Ujjain.

Under the Viceroys there was a host of functionaries, concerning whom we hear a good deal in the Edicts, as well as in the writings of the Greek authors and Chāṇakya. Space will not permit of an elaborate analysis of the information recorded, but we may note that the Edicts disclose the existence of high officers called Rājūkas, or Commissioners, set over hundreds of thousands of souls, Prādesikas, or District Officers of lower rank, and a multitude of officials grouped together under the generic title of *mahāmātras*. The sovereign exercised a personal supervision over all these grades through his Agents, or 'men,' who, perhaps, should be identified with the *episkopoi*, or 'overseers,' of Megasthenes. The intensely personal nature of the government is brought before us vividly in Rock Edict VI., which exhibits Asoka wrestling with a task beyond the power of man. The authorities give us glimpses of various Departments of the Government, including one concerned with irrigation, and it is clear that the State was highly organized for both civil and military purposes.

The mainstay of the Treasury was the land-revenue, or government share, normally one fourth, of the produce, but it was supplemented by a great variety of other dues and taxes. The most profitable of these was the tax on goods sold, which was the subject of elaborate regulations and was levied with stern severity. Certain evasions of the revenue were even punishable with death.

The criminal law did not err on the side of mercy, death or mutilation being freely inflicted for various offences. Asoka takes great credit to himself for allowing condemned criminals a respite of three days between sentence and execution in order to give to them time for pious meditation and to their friends opportunities for works of charity, but he does not claim to have mitigated the severity of the substantive law. In the Provincials' Edict he warns his officials in the newly-annexed province of Kalinga to protect the people from imprisonment or ill-usage inflicted without just cause. The oppression practised by subordinate officials is no novelty in India, and Asoka, notwithstanding his despotic power, was not always able to ensure the practical application of the excellent sermons which he took so much trouble to preach.

The capital, Pāṭaliputra (the modern Patna and Bankipore), which had been founded about 500 B.C., is mentioned twice in the Edicts (Rock Edict V. and Sārnāth Pillar) by name, and is indirectly referred to in other passages. We know from external sources that it was a splendid city, situated on the northern bank of the Sōn, which then joined the Ganges lower down, that it was strongly fortified, and replete with the commodities and luxuries befitting the headquarters of a mighty monarch. It was governed by six Departmental Boards, and presumably the other cities of the empire were administered on similar lines. The Edicts refer to the officers in charge of several towns, Tosalī, Samāpā, and Isila, besides the Princes already mentioned. The Sovereign evidently was in a position to enforce his commands even in distant cities like Ujjain and Taxila.

This observation leads us to notice the system of communication. Megasthenes tells of the Grand Trunk Road which ran from the capital to the north-western frontier, marked with pillars at every half-*kōs*, or about a mile and a quarter, and Asoka was very proud of the measures which he took for the comfort and convenience of travellers, as enumerated in Rock Edict II. and section V. of Pillar Edict VII. Notwithstanding the rather inconvenient position of the capital in the east, it is plain that communication between the different parts of the empire was well maintained by road and river.

The political organization which enabled the Maurya Sovereigns for three generations during ninety years to administer an enormous empire with success well deserves attention, but the world's interest in the dynasty is mainly concentrated upon Asoka as a moral teacher and the man who raised Buddhism from the position of a local Indian sect to that of one of the chief religions of the world. From that point of view his personal history is a matter of high importance, and every step which he took on the road to wisdom as he knew it has had its effect on the development of mankind.

Until recently writers on Buddhism were accustomed to approach the history of Asoka through the traditions recorded many centuries after his death in the chronicles of Ceylon, and so found themselves entangled in a mass of mythological fable. But people are beginning to acknowledge that the primary authority for his life is his autobiography as recorded in his inscriptions, and that the traditional sources of knowledge are of secondary value, not to be despised, but still far inferior to his personal testimony. Time has been required to ascertain the true meaning of the epigraphic record, but the difficulties have now been solved for the most part, although some still remain, and we are able to obtain a fairly complete notion of Asoka's positive teaching and of the gradual development of the ideas which his great political power enabled him to impose upon a large section of mankind. We shall, therefore, try to ascertain what he tells us about himself, his thoughts, and his work. The inscriptions bear so many marks of the Sovereign's personality that we may safely treat them as being in substance his writings.

The only epigraphic document in India containing the name of Asoka is the inscription dated 150 A.D. of the Western Satrap Rudradāman, which commemorates the repair of the embankment of a lake at Girnār in Kāṭhiāwāṛ, originally 'ordered to be made by the Vaiśya Pushyagupta, the provincial governor of the Maurya king Chandragupta; and adorned with conduits for Asoka Maurya by the Yavana Rājā Tushāspha during his rule.' This incidental reference to the Maurya kings is of value as a confirmation of the literary traditional history of the dynasty and as clear proof that Chandragupta's authority extended over the peninsula of Kaṭhiāwāṛ in the far west.

Asoka's full name, as recorded in the Purānas, was Asoka-vardhana, but in his inscriptions he never uses his personal name, and is content to describe himself by official hereditary titles, which in their fullest form (*Devānaṃpiya Piyadasi Rājā*) may be best rendered by the phrase 'His Sacred and Gracious Majesty the King,' combining the old Tudor and Stuart styles. The opening of Rock Edict VIII. affords clear proof that Asoka's predecessors were known as 'Their Sacred Majesties' (*Devānaṃpiya*), and the title Piyadassana, an alternative for Piyadasi met with in the chronicles of Ceylon, is applied in the *Mudrārākshasa* play to Chandragupta Maurya. When the title *Piyadasi* is combined with *Rājā* only, the Tudor expression 'The King's Grace' or 'His Grace the King' is a good equivalent. The reader must be asked to accept the assurance that the identity of Asoka of the Ceylonese chronicles and Puranic lists with the author of the inscriptions translated in this volume has been conclusively established. The detailed proof will be found in two articles in the *J.R.A.S.* for 1901.

The chronological position of the Maurya dynasty is determined mainly by the synchronisms of Chandragupta with Seleucus Nicator and of Asoka with Antiochus Theos, grandson of Seleucus, and the other Hellenistic Kings mentioned in Rock Edict XIII. Some help in settling the question being obtained from other sources, the result is that the accession of Asoka to the throne may be placed in 273, his consecration (*abhisheka*) in 269, and his death in 232 B.C. Absolute precision in dates is unattainable for various reasons, one of which is that we do not know the month or season in which the accession, consecration, or death occurred. The maximum possible error in any of the three dates may be taken as two years. Asoka's records when dated at all are dated according to 'regnal years' reckoned from his consecration in 269 B.C. We do not know why his formal consecration, the ceremony equivalent to coronation, was delayed for four years. The tales on the subject in the Ceylonese chronicles are mere legends and folk-lore. Perhaps the true explanation may be found in the remark of Mr. R. Shamasastry that 'it seems likely that in ancient India it was the custom to instal or consecrate a king or patriarch once at the close of every cycle of four years' (*Gavām Ayana, the Vedic Era*, Mysore, 1908, p. 119). Now, after these preliminary explanations, we are in a position to see what Asoka has to say about himself.

Literary tradition represents him as being Viceroy of Ujjain when his father died, and he is said to have been Viceroy at Taxila also. These statements may be accepted, for we know from the edicts that both the cities named were the seats of governments administered by princes of the imperial family. The stories which relate the slaughter of ninety-nine brothers by Asoka to clear his way to the throne and ascribe fiendish wickedness to him in his early years are mere monkish fables, invented with a purpose. The truth seems to be that in those years he lived the life of an ordinary Hindu King of his age. Whether or not he waged any wars in the first period of his reign we do not know; if he did, he makes no allusion to them, nor does tradition. But we know from his own words (Rock Edict I.) that he indulged freely in meat and permitted the daily slaughter of animals for use in the imperial kitchen on an enormous scale, that he followed the chase as his grandfather had done, that he sanctioned animal sacrifices, and allowed the celebration at the capital and elsewhere of feasts accompanied by the drinking of liquor and merry-making of various kinds. There is no indication that he had to repent of anything worse than such practices of the Rājās of his age.

But in the ninth year after his consecration (*i.e.* in 261 B.C.) he conquered and annexed Kalinga, the province on the coast of the Bay of Bengal, corresponding to the Ganjām District and part of Orissa. The horrors of war which he then witnessed deeply impressed his conscience, and he was led, probably by his teacher Upagupta, whose memory is preserved in the northern traditions, to forswear war and to devote his whole energy and imperial power to the teaching and propagation of *Dharma*, the rule of life, as understood in a Buddhist sense. His 'profound sorrow and regret' for the miseries caused by his ambition are recorded in Rock Edict XIII. in burning words which plainly came from his heart, and he advised his successors to abstain from conquests made by arms and to content themselves with the 'true conquest' effected by the Law of Piety.

The *Dharma*, or Law of Piety, preached by Asoka for nearly thirty years, was not merely 'the ordinary *dharma* of Kings,' as practised by his hunting, sacrificing, merry-making forefathers, but was a specially Buddhist modification of the Hindu ideal of duty. The two virtues placed in the forefront were reverence to all persons deserving of it by reason of rank, age, or station, and the extremest regard for the sanctity of animal life. Both these requirements are so vigorously insisted on in the Edicts that it is hard to say which he considered the more important, but, perhaps, the sanctity of animal life interested him more than anything else.

A full discussion of the imperial teaching would require more space than can be given here, and it will suffice perhaps to summarize it in words which I have used elsewhere:—

'The Edicts reveal Asoka as a man who sought to combine the piety of the monk with the wisdom of the King, and to make India the kingdom of righteousness as he conceived it, a theocracy without a God; in which the government should act the part of Providence, and guide the people in the right way. Every man, he maintained, must work out his own salvation, and eat the fruit of his deeds. "The fruit of exertion is not to be attained by a great man only; because even by the small man who chooses to exert himself immense heavenly bliss may be won." For this purpose has this precept been proclaimed:—"Let small and great exert themselves to this end." The government could point out the road, but each man must travel it for himself.

Reverence, compassion, truthfulness, and sympathy were the virtues which he inculcated; irreverence, cruelty, falsehood, and intolerance were the vices which he condemned.'

The Edicts give many slightly variant summaries of the Law of Piety, which will be found in Minor Rock Edict II.; Rock Edicts III., IV., VII., IX., XI., XIII.; and Pillar Edicts III. and VII.

Asoka's teaching is confined to a purely practical code of morals, which is not based on any metaphysical or theological theory. The only foundation laid is the word of the Buddha, 'Whatsoever, Reverend Sirs,' observes the imperial preacher when specially addressing the monks and nuns, 'has been said by the Venerable Buddha, all of that has been well said.' The inducements held out to men to follow 'The Way of the Church' are the hope of winning both the imperial favour and heavenly bliss. The Edicts are full of references to 'the next world,' the 'beyond.' How Asoka's ideas on this subject are to be reconciled with the official doctrine of the books is a matter which cannot be discussed here. It is certain that Asoka makes no allusion to either Nirvāna or the *Karma* doctrine which affirms the transmission of merit or demerit from one existence to another. Nevertheless, it is also certain that Asoka studied Buddhist works closely resembling the existing Pāli Canon, for out of seven long passages cited in the Bhābrā Edict as the Emperor's favourites, five have been identified in the Nikāya portion of the Canon, and the other short text which Asoka specially fancied occurs in at least two places in the scriptures.

The Minor Pillar Edicts, and especially the newly discovered one from Sārnāth, prove that the Church was highly organized and that its discipline was closely regulated by the Emperor in person as Head of the Church and Defender of the Faith.

Asoka's gradual progress in the faith is traced in his autobiography. Immediately after the Kalinga war his remorse led him to love, protect, and proclaim the Law of Piety (Rock Edict XIII.), and about the same time, that is to say in his 9th 'regnal year,' 261 B.C., he became a lay disciple, and so remained for about two and a half years, without exerting himself strenuously. Then his zeal was quickened, and he joined the Order as a monk, exerting himself strenuously for more than a year. These indications bring us to his 13th 'regnal year,' 257 B.C., when he began the practice of inscribing the Law of Piety in imperishable characters on rocks and pillars so that 'the Good Law might long endure' (Minor Rock Edict I., Pillar Edict VI., Bhābrā Edict). During his period of strenuous exertion (259 to 257 B.C.) he abolished the Royal Hunt, substituting for it 'pious tours' (Rock Edict VIII.), and apparently went himself on such a tour with energy so great that he changed his abode 256 times in the space of a year and some months (Minor Rock Edict I.).

Missionaries were sent to all parts of India, to Ceylon, and even to the distant realms of Antiochus Theos, King of Syria; Ptolemy Philadelphus, King of Egypt; Magas, King of Cyrene; Antigonus Gonatas, King of Macedonia; and Alexander, King of Epirus, with instructions to disseminate the teachings of the Law of Piety, the Buddhist *dharma*, in all those countries. They were also charged to diffuse the knowledge of remedies useful for the bodily healing of both men and beasts (Rock Edicts II., XIII.); and in his own dominions Asoka was careful to secure an ample supply of such remedies and to make liberal provision for the care and comfort of the sick, as well as for the convenience of travellers (Pillar Edict VII.). Such arrangements were then unknown, and even Christian nations neglected to take any thought for matters of the kind until many centuries later. The effect of Asoka's missions in making Buddhism one of the great religions of the world has been noticed already and is too large a subject for further discussion in this place.

For the machinery required to promulgate his teaching within the empire Asoka relied largely on the quinquennial circuits which his officers were required to make by orders passed in the 13th 'regnal year,' 257 B.C. In the provinces of Ujjain and Taxila the circuits were ordered to be triennial (Rock Edict III., Kalinga Provincials' Edict). During their travels officials were enjoined to busy themselves with preaching, while not neglecting the ordinary duties of administration.

In the 14th 'regnal year,' 256 B.C. he instituted a class of special high officers, *Dharmamahāmātras*, or Censors, charged with the duty of strictly enforcing the rules of the Law of Piety. Commissioners (Rājūkas) also were appointed, and a system of close espionage over all classes of the population, including the women, was organized and carried out by a swarm of officials. The interference with personal liberty must have been great, and it is not surprising that when Asoka died a reaction occurred and his system disappeared.

The publication of the Fourteen Rock Edicts, which seems to have taken place in the 14th 'regnal year,' 256 B.C., was soon followed by that of the Kalinga Edicts. The other great series of orders, the Seven Pillar Edicts, belongs to the 27th and 28th 'regnal years,' 243 and 242 B.C. The Minor

Pillar Edicts must be of later date, and it seems probable that their issue was connected with the resolutions of the Buddhist Council held at Pāṭaliputra, which is not mentioned in the Edicts, but is attested by literary tradition. If so, the Council must have been held between 242 and 232 B.C. The Tarāi inscriptions commemorate visits to the holy places of Buddhism in the 21st 'regnal year,' 249 B.C., and the Cave dedications in the Barābar Hills were made in the 13th and 20th 'regnal years,' equivalent to 257 and 250 B.C. The dedication of exceedingly costly works to the use of the Ājīvika ascetics, whom some Buddhist writers regarded as beyond the pale of salvation, is a striking exemplification of the toleration taught in Rock Edict XII. The exultation expressed in Minor Rock Edict I. over the fall of the Brahmans and their gods is in a different spirit, and seems to indicate that in the first glow of enthusiasm for his new creed Asoka had not attained to the more philosophical attitude adopted a little later.

There can be no doubt that Asoka really joined the monastic Order in the 11th or 12th 'regnal year,' 263 or 262 B.C., and that notwithstanding that step, he retained his grasp of the imperial sceptre, and combined the control of the empire with the government of the Church. His latest known records, the Minor Pillar Edicts, exhibit him in the double capacity of Emperor and Head of the Church, as also does the Bhābrā Edict, which belongs probably to a much earlier period. The Queen's Edict—one of the late Minor Pillar Edicts—speaks of his two queens and a son named Tīvara, without any indication that he had abandoned the family life. Earlier documents also refer to his wives and descendants. How he managed to reconcile the roles of monk and King is not clear, but the difficulty is partly explained by the fact that Buddhist 'ordination' does not exact an irrevocable vow, and that in modern Burma men pass freely from the monastic to the secular life, and back again, as they please. The legend of Vītāsoka, the King's brother, who was provided with a hermitage in the palace grounds, shows that it was possible for a member of the royal family to comply with the rules of the Order sufficiently without leaving the palace precincts, and Buddhist literature contains many passages recommending deference to the wishes of Kings. The ecclesiastical authorities were not likely to find fault with the orthodoxy of the arrangements made by their lord and master. Further light is thrown upon the apparent difficulty by the case of the Chinese

Emperor, Hsiao Yen, alias Wu ti, the first of the Liang Dynasty, who 'was a devout Buddhist, living upon priestly fare and taking only one meal a day, and on two occasions, in 527 and 529, he actually adopted the priestly garb. He also wrote a Buddhist ritual in ten books. Interpreting the Buddhist commandment "Thou shalt not kill" in its strictest sense, he caused the sacrificial victims to be made of dough' (Giles, *Chinese Literature*, p. 133).* What the Chinese Emperor could do Asoka could do, and, however he managed the details, it is certain that Asoka became a monk some four ($2\frac{1}{2}+1$ and a fraction) years after he first took up the cult of *Dharma* on the conclusion of the Kalinga war, and, nevertheless, retained his position and power as Emperor, certainly up to about 240 B.C., and probably until his death. I cannot find any sufficient reason for believing that he ever abdicated. Where and how he died we have no knowledge.

A brief notice of the position, distribution, script, language, and style of the Asoka inscriptions may conclude this Introduction.

The Minor Rock Edicts, assumed in accordance with the opinion of M. Senart and Mr. F. W. Thomas to be the earliest, are found at the following places:—

(1) Bairāt in Jaypur State, Rājputāna.
(2) Rūpnāth in Jabalpur District, Central Provinces, 14 miles W. of Sleemanabad railway station.
(3) Sahasrām in Shahabad District, S. Bihār.
(4-6) At and near Siddāpura in Mysore (three copies).

The Bhābrā Edict also is at Bairāt.

The Fourteen Rock Edicts, more or less complete, occur at seven sites, namely:—

(1) Shāhbāzgarhi, in Yūsufzai country, 40 miles N.E. of Peshāwar.
(2) Mānsahra in the Hazāra District, N.W. Frontier Province.
(3) Kālsī in Dehra Dūn District, U.P.
(4) Sopāra in Thāna District, Bombay.
(5) Girnār in Jūnāgaṛh State, Kāṭhiāwāṛ.
(6) Dhauli in Purī District, Orissa, near Bhuvaneśvar.
(7) Jaugaḍa in Ganjām District, Madras, W.N.W. from Ganjām town.

* *For further details see Du Halde*, HIST. OF CHINA, *Engl. transl.*, *3rd ed.*, 1741, *vol. I.*, *p.* 381.

The Kalinga Edicts also are at Dhauli and Jaugaḍa.

The seventh Pillar Edict exists on the Delhi-Topra Pillar only; the first six Edicts occur there and at five other places, six in all, namely:—

(1) Delhi, on the Kothila, removed from Topra in Ambāla District, Panjāb.

(2) Delhi, on the Ridge, removed from Mīrath (Meerut), U.P.

(3) Allahabad, U.P. The pillar almost certainly was transported from the Buddhist Kauśāmbī, which probably lay about 90 miles S.W. of Allahabad.

(4) Lauṛiyā-Ararāj, in Champāran District, N. Bihār.

(5) Lauṛiyā-Nandangaṛh, 15 miles N.N.W. of Bettia in the same District.

(6) Rāmpurwā, near Pipariā in N.E. corner of the same District.

Of the Minor Pillar Edicts, two, the Kauśāmbī and the Queen's, are on the Allahabad Pillar. The Sānchi Edict is on a pillar at Sānchi in the Bhopāl State, Central India, and the Sārnāth Edict is on a pillar at Sārnāth, about 3½ miles to the north of Benares.

The Tarāi Commemorative Inscriptions are on pillars in the Nepalese Tarāi to the north of the Bastī District, U.P., at Rummindcī, and at Niglīva, some thirteen miles to the N.W. of that site.

The Cave Dedications of Asoka are in the Barābar Hills of the Gayā District, S. Bihār.

The Cave Dedications of Asoka's grandson Daśaratha are about a mile distant from the Barābar inscriptions.

No Asoka inscriptions have yet been found in Bengal east of Bihār or in Sind, but those known are scattered over the rest of India from the Himalaya to Mysore, and from the Arabian Sea to the Bay of Bengal. Including Daśaratha's dedications the number of distinct documents may be reckoned as about forty. The seventh Pillar Edict, devoted to a review of the imperial measures taken for the promotion of piety, alludes to several of the earlier documents.

All the inscriptions are composed in one or other dialect of Prakrit, that is to say in vernaculars nearly allied to the recognized literary languages, Sanskrit, Pāli, and the Prakrit of books, but not identical with any of them. Many words not known to occur elsewhere are met with in the Asoka inscriptions, and this fact causes difficulties of interpretation. Most of the documents are in the dialect of Magadha, the province in which the capital was situated.

The two sets of inscriptions on the north-western frontier at Mānsahra and Shāhbāzgarhi are inscribed in the script called Kharoshṭhī, which was written from right to left like Hebrew, and was a form of the Aramaic character introduced by the officials of the Persian government who administered the frontier regions before the time of Alexander the Great.

All the other inscriptions are incised in varieties of the ancient Brāhmī character, read from left to right, which was the parent of the Devanāgarī and most of the Indian alphabets. But at Siddāpura one word of the scribe's signature is written in Kharoshṭhī, the official apparently having been imported from the north. The phrasing of the edicts varies considerably in different recensions, and occasionally the variations are material, affecting the sense. The different copies of the first six Pillar Edicts agree with one another almost exactly.

The earlier interpreters passed severe criticisms on the style of the edicts, which was supposed to be excessively awkward and obscure, betraying lack of practice in prose composition. But such criticism no longer holds good. The publication of accurate facsimiles has settled the text in multitudes of passages which were long misunderstood, and the advances made of late years in linguistic and grammatical knowledge enable the translator to avoid many of the awkward turns of expression which seemed unavoidable to the early workers at the subject. It is true that many of the inscriptions are, as their author freely admits in Rock Edict XIV., full of repetitions which jar on the ear of the European reader, but such repetitions are even still more prominent in the Buddhist Pāli Canon, and were the result of Asoka's deliberate choice. They are not indications of want of skill of composition. It is also true that in a few of the documents elliptical forms of expression are used, and that in some, especially in the Kalinga Edicts, abrupt changes from *oratio obliqua* to *oratio directa* are made which present some difficulty in translation. But such transitions obviously are made with the intention of quoting Asoka's own words as far as possible, and really indicate considerable skill in the literary use of language. I believe that Asoka and his secretaries were well accustomed to prose composition, and am disposed to believe that a knowledge of reading and writing was more widely diffused in the country than it now is in the more backward provinces. The numerous communities of Buddhist monks probably kept schools as they now do in

Burma, through which a large part of the population passed. Nuns evidently were numerous, and so the females shared in the benefits of education.

The style of many of the Edicts is not wanting in simple dignity and power. My readers can decide for themselves how far this judgment is justified. The versions in this volume closely follow the texts, but the translator has not been unmindful of the precepts of Goethe, who laid down in wise words the principles of translation, as follows :—

'In so far as every language has a peculiar genius, a literal translation must necessarily be a bad one; and any faithful translation will of its nature be free. In other words, a translator will err if he slavishly adheres to mere expression ; he must have complete liberty to give his author's meaning and style in the manner which he holds to be truest to the original ; and so, in translating from a foreign tongue, it will be well for him to have some knowledge of his own. . . . The best translation is thus a re-embodiment of the author's spirit—a real metempsychosis.'*

I hope that the readers of the following pages may find in them a re-embodiment of the spirit of the Buddhist Sovereign of India twenty-two centuries ago.

* *Goethe*, MAXIMS, *transl. Bailey Saunders*, *p.* 54.

THE EDICTS OF ASOKA

EDICTS AND INSCRIPTIONS.

THE MINOR ROCK EDICTS.

EDICT I. (Rūpnāth Text). See next.

THE FRUIT OF EXERTION.

'Thus saith his Sacred Majesty:--

For more than two years and a half I was a lay disciple, without, however, exerting myself strenuously. But it is more than a year since I joined the Order and have exerted myself strenuously. During that time the gods who were regarded as true all over India have been shown to be untrue.

For this is the fruit of exertion. Nor is this to be attained by a great man only, because even by the small man who exerts himself immense heavenly bliss may be won.

And for this purpose has the precept been composed:--

"Let small and great exert themselves." My neighbours, too, should learn this lesson; and may such exertion long endure!

And this purpose will grow--yea, it will grow immensely--at least one-and-a-half fold will it increase in growth. And this purpose must be written on the rocks, both afar off and here, and wherever there is a stone pillar it must be written on the stone pillar.

And, according to this text, so far as your jurisdiction extends, you must send it out everywhere. By the 'Traveller' was the precept composed. 256 changes of abode of the Sata (or 'of Satas').'

THE MINOR ROCK EDICTS.

The same Edict (Brahmagiri Text). See preceding.

The same Subject.

'By command of the Prince and officers at Suvarnagiri, the officers at Isila are to be addressed with greetings and further addressed as follows:--

These are the instructions of His Sacred Majesty:--

For more than two years and a half I was a lay disciple, without, however, exerting myself strenuously. But a year, in fact, more than a year, ago I joined the Order, and since then have exerted myself strenuously. During that time the men who were, all over India, regarded as true, have been, with their gods, shown to be untrue.

For this is the fruit of exertion. Nor is this to be attained by a great man only, because even by the small man who chooses to exert himself, immense heavenly bliss may be won.

For this purpose has this precept been proclaimed:--"Let small and great exert themselves to this end."

My neighbours too should learn this lesson, and may such exertion long endure!

And this purpose will grow--yea, it will grow immensely--at least one-and-a-half fōld will it increase in growth.

And the precept quoted above was proclaimed by the 'Traveller' 256 [times ?].'

MINOR ROCK EDICTS.

EDICT II.

SUMMARY OF THE LAW OF PIETY.

'Thus saith His Sacred Majesty:--

Father and mother must be hearkened to; similarly, respect for living creatures must be firmly established; truth must be spoken. These are the virtues of the Law of Piety which must be practised. Similarly, the teacher must be reverenced by the pupil, and towards relations fitting courtesy should be shown.

This is the ancient nature (of piety)--this leads to length of days, and according to this men must act.'

Written by Paḍa the scribe.

THE BHĀBRĀ EDICT.

ASOKA'S FAVOURITE PASSAGES OF SCRIPTURE.

'His Grace the King of Magadha addresses the Church with greetings and bids its members prosperity and good health.

You know, Reverend Sirs, how far extend my respect for and faith in the Buddha, the Sacred Law, and the Church.

Whatsoever, Reverend Sirs, has been said by the Venerable Buddha all of that has been well said.

However, Reverend Sirs, if on my own account I may point out (a particular text), I venture to adduce this one:--"Thus the Good Law will long endure."

Reverend Sirs, these passages of the Law, to wit,

The Exaltation of Vinaya;

The Supernatural Powers of the Aryas;

Fears of what may happen;

The Song of the Hermit;

The Dialogue on the Hermit's Life;

The Questioning of Upatishya; and

The Address to Rāhula beginning with the subject of Falsehood--

spoken by the Venerable Buddha--these passages of the Law, Reverend Sirs, I desire that many monks and nuns should frequently hear and meditate--and that likewise the laity, male and female, should do the same.

For this reason, Reverend Sirs, I am causing this to be written, so that people may know my wishes.'

ROCK EDICT I.

THE SACREDNESS OF LIFE.

'This pious edict has been written by command of His Sacred and Gracious Majesty the King.

Here (in the capital) no animal may be slaughtered for sacrifice, nor may holiday-feasts be held, because His Sacred and Gracious Majesty the King sees manifōld evil in holiday-fēasts, although holiday-fēasts in certain places are meritorious in the sight of His Sacred and Gracious Majesty the King.

Formerly, in the Kitchen of His Sacred and Gracious Majesty the King from day to day many hundred thousands of living creatures were slaughtered for savoury meats. But now, when this pious edict is being written, there are slaughtered (daily) for savoury meats only three living creatures, to wit, two peacocks and one antelope--the antelope, however, not invariably. Even these three living creatures in future shall not be slaughtered.'

ROCK EDICT II.

PROVISION OF COMFORTS FOR MEN AND ANIMALS.

'Everywhere in the Dominions of His Sacred and Gracious Majesty the King--as well as among his neighbours--such as the Cholas, Pāndyas, Satiyaputra, Ketalaputra, Ceylon, Antiochus the Greek king, and likewise the kings near unto that Antiochus--everywhere has His Sacred and Gracious Majesty the King made two kinds of curative arrangements, to wit, curative arrangements for men and curative arrangements for beasts. Medicinal herbs also, medicinal for man and medicinal for beast, wherever they were lacking, have been imported and planted; roots also and fruits, wherever they were lacking, everywhere have been imported and planted.

On the roads both wells have been dug and trees planted for the enjoyment of man and beast.'

ROCK EDICT III.

THE QUINQUENNIAL CIRCUIT.

'Thus saith His Sacred and Gracious Majesty the King:--When I had been consecrated twelve years I issued this command:--

Everywhere in my dominions the (subordinate) officials, and the Commissioners, and the District officers every five years must proceed on circuit, as well for their other duties, as for this special purpose, namely, to proclaim the Law of Piety, to wit, 'A meritorious thing is the hearkening to father and mother; a meritorious thing is liberality to friends, acquaintances, relatives, Brahmans, and ascetics; a meritorious thing it is to abstain from slaughter of living creatures; a meritorious thing it is to spend little and store little.'

Let the (monastic) communities also appoint officials for the reckoning with regard to both the objects and the accounts (or, 'in accordance with reason and specific instructions').'

ROCK EDICT IV.

THE PRACTICE OF PIETY.

'For a long time past, even for many hundred years, the slaughter of living creatures, cruelty to animate beings, disrespect to relatives, and disrespect to Brahmans and ascetics have grown.

But now, by reason of the practice of piety by His Sacred and Gracious Majesty the King, instead of the sound of the war-drum the sound of the drum of piety is heard, while heavenly spectacles of processional cars, elephants, illuminations, and the like, are displayed to the people.

As for many hundred years past has not happened, at this present, by reason of the proclamation of the Law of Piety by His Sacred and Gracious Majesty the King, the cessation of slaughter of living creatures, the prevention of cruelty to animate beings, respect to relatives, respect to Brahmans and ascetics, hearkening to father and mother, and hearkening to elders are growing.

Thus, and in many other ways, the practice of piety is growing, and His Sacred and Gracious Majesty the King will cause that practice of piety to grow still more.

The sons, grandsons, and great-grandsons of His Sacred and Gracious Majesty the King will promote the growth of that practice until the end of the cycle, and, abiding in piety and morality, will proclaim the Law of Piety. For this is the best of

all deeds, the proclamation of the Law of Piety, and the practice of piety is not for the immoral man.
In this matter growth is meritorious, and not to decrease is meritorious.
For this very purpose has this writing been made, in order that men in this matter may strive for growth and not suffer decrease.
This has been written by command of His Sacred and Gracious Majesty the King after he had been consecrated twelve years.'

ROCK EDICT V.

CENSORS OF THE LAW OF PIETY.

'Thus saith His Sacred and Gracious Majesty the King:--A good deed is a difficult thing. Now by me many good deeds have been done. He who performs a good deed does a difficult thing. Should my sons, grandsons, and my descendants after them until the end of the cycle follow in this path, they will do well; but in this matter, should a man neglect the commandment, he will do ill, because sin is an easy thing.
Now in all the long ages past, officers known as Censors of the Law of Piety never had been appointed, whereas by me, after I had been consecrated thirteen years, Censors of the Law of Piety were made.

Among people of all denominations they are engaged in promoting the establishment of piety, the progress of piety, and the welfare and happiness of the lieges, as well as of the Yonas, Kambojas, Gandhāras, Rāshtrikas, Pitenikas, and other nations on my borders.

They are engaged in promoting the welfāre and happiness of servants and masters, of Brahmans and the rich, of the poor, and of the aged, as well as in removing hindrances from the path of the lieges.

They are engaged in the prevention of wrongful imprisonment or chastisement, in the work of removing hindrances and of deliverance, considering cases where a man has a large family, has been smitten by calamity, or is advanced in years.

Here, at Pātaliputra, and in all the provincial towns they are everywhere engaged in supervising the fēmale establishments of my brothers and sisters and other relatives.

Everywhere in my loyal empire these Censors of the Law of Piety are engaged with those among my lieges who are devoted to piety, established in piety, or addicted to almsgiving.

For this purpose has this pious edict been written, that it may endure for long, and that my subjects may act accordingly.'

ROCK EDICT VI.

THE PROMPT DISPATCH OF BUSINESS.

'Thus saith His Sacred and Gracious Majesty the King:--During long ages past business has not been disposed of, nor have reports been received at all hours. Now by me this arrangement has been made that at all hours and in all places--whether I am dining, or in the ladies' apartments, or in my bedroom, or in my closet, or in my carriage, or in the palace-gardens--the official reporters should report to me on the people's business. At all places I am ready to dispose of the people's business.

And if, perchance, I personally by word of mouth command that a gift be made or order executed, or anything urgent is entrusted to the officials, and in that business a dispute arises or fraud occurs among the communities, I have commanded that immediate report be made to me at any hour and at any place, for I am never fully satisfied with my efforts and my dispatch of business.

Work I must for the welfare of all, and the root of the matter is in effort and the dispatch of business, for nothing is more efficacious to secure the welfare of all. And for what do I toil? For no other end than this, that I may discharge my debt to animate beings, and that while I make some happy here, they may in the next world gain heaven.

For this purpose have I caused this pious edict to be written, that it may long endure, and that my sons, grandsons, and great-grandsons may strive for the welfare of all. That, however, is a difficult thing, save by the utmost exertion.

ROCK EDICT VII.

IMPERFECT FULFILMENT OF THE LAW.

'His Sacred and Gracious Majesty the King desires that in all places men of every denomination may abide, for they all desire mastery over the senses and purity of mind.

Man, however, is various in his wishes, and various in his likings.

Some of the denominations will perform the whole, others will perform but one part of the commandment. Even for a person to whom lavish liberality is impossible, the virtues of mastery over the senses, purity of mind, gratitude, and steadfastness are altogether indispensable.'

ROCK EDICT VIII.

PIOUS TOURS.

'In times past Their Sacred Majesties used to go out on so-called "tours of pleasure," during which hunting and other similar amusements used to be practised.

His Sacred and Gracious Majesty the King, however, after he had been consecrated ten years, went forth on the road to wisdom. Thus originated the "tours of piety" (dharma), wherein are practised the visiting of ascetics and Brahmans, with liberality to them, the visiting of elders, with largess of gold, the visiting of the country and the people, with instruction in the Law of Piety and discussion of the Law of Piety.

Consequently, since that time these are the pleasures of His Sacred and Gracious Majesty the King in exchange for those of the past.'

ROCK EDICT IX.

TRUE CEREMONIAL.

'Thus saith His Sacred and Gracious Majesty the King:--

People perform various ceremonies on occasions of sickness, the weddings of sons, the weddings of daughters, the birth of children, and departure on journeys. On these and other similar occasions people perform various ceremonies. But at such times the womankind perform many, manifold, trivial, and worthless ceremonies.

Ceremonies certainly have to be performed, although that sort bears little fruit. This sort, however--the ceremonial of piety--bears great fruit. In it are included proper treatment of slaves and servants, honour to teachers, gentleness towards living creatures, and liberality towards ascetics and Brahmans. These things, and others of the same kind, are called the ceremonial of piety.

Therefore ought a father, son, brother, master, friend, or comrade, nay, even a neighbour to say, "This is meritorious, this is the ceremonial to be performed until the attainment of the desired end." By what sort of ceremonies is the desired end attained? for the ceremonial of this world is of doubtful efficacy; perchance it may accomplish the desired end, perchance it may not, and its effect is merely of this world.

The ceremonial of piety, on the contrary, is not temporal; for even if it fails to attain the desired end in this world, it certainly begets endless merit in the other world. If it happens to attain the desired end, then a gain of two kinds is assured, namely, in this world the desired end, and in the other world the begetting of endless merit through the aforesaid ceremonial of piety.'

ROCK EDICT X.

TRUE GLORY.

'His Sacred and Gracious Majesty the King does not believe that glory or renown brings much profit unless in both the present and the future my people obediently hearken to the Law of Piety and conform to its precepts. For that purpose only does His

Sacred and Gracious Majesty the King desire glory or renown.

Whatsoever exertions His Sacred and Gracious Majesty the King makes, all are for the sake of the life hereafter, so that every one may be freed from peril, and that peril is vice.

Difficult, verily, it is to attain such freedom, whether by people of low or of high degree, save by the utmost exertion, with giving up all other aims. That, however, for him of high degree is difficult.'

ROCK EDICT XI.

TRUE ALMSGIVING.

'Thus saith his Sacred and Gracious Majesty the King:

There is no such almsgiving as is the almsgiving of the Law of Piety--friendship in piety, the distribution of piety, kinship in piety. Herein does it consist--in proper treatment of slaves and servants, hearkening to father and mother, giving to friends, comrades, relations, ascetics, and Brahmans, and sparing of living creatures. Therefore a father, son, brother, master, friend, comrade, nay, even a neighbour, ought to say, "This is meritorious, this ought to be done."

He who acts thus both gains this world and in the other world begets infinite virtue, by means of this very almsgiving of piety.'

ROCK EDICT XII.

TOLERATION.

'His Sacred and Gracious Majesty the King does reverence to men of all sects, whether ascetics or householders, by gifts and various forms of reverence.

His Sacred Majesty, however, cares not so much for gifts or external reverence as that there should be a growth of the essence of the matter in all sects. The growth of the essence of the matter assumes various forms, but the root of it is restraint of speech, to wit, a man must not do reverence to his own sect or disparage that of another man without reason. Depreciation should be for specific reasons only, because the sects of other people all deserve reverence for one reason or another.

By thus acting, a man exalts his own sect, and at the same time does service to the sects of other people. By acting contrariwise, a man hurts his own sect, and does disservice to the sects of other people. For he who does reverence to his own sect while disparaging the sects of others wholly from attachment to his own, with intent to enhance the splendour of his own sect, in reality by such conduct inflicts the severest injury on his own sect.

Concord, therefore, is meritorious, to wit, hearkening and hearkening willingly to the Law of Piety as accepted by other people. For this is the desire of His Sacred Majesty that all sects should hear much teaching and hold sound doctrine.

Wherefore the adherents of all sects, whatever they may be, must be informed that His Sacred Majesty cares not so much for gifts or external reverence as that there should be growth in the essence of the matter and respect for all sects.
For this very purpose are employed the Censors of the Law of Piety, the Censors of the Women, the (?) Inspectors, and other official bodies. And this is the fruit thereof--the growth of one's own sect, and the enhancement of the splendour of the Law of Piety.'

ROCK EDICT XIII.

TRUE CONQUEST.

The Kalingas were conquered by His Sacred and Gracious Majesty the King when he had been consecrated eight years. One hundred and fifty thousand persons were thence carried away captive, one hundred thousand were there slain, and many times that number perished.
Directly after the annexation of the Kalingas, began His Sacred Majesty's zealous protection of the Law of Piety, his love of that Law, and his giving instruction in that Law (dharma). Thus arose His Sacred Majesty's remorse for having conquered the Kalingas, because the conquest of a country previously unconquered involves the slaughter, death, and carrying away captive of the people. That is a

matter of profound sorrow and regret to His Sacred Majesty.

There is, however, another reason for His Sacred Majesty feeling still more regret, inasmuch as in such a country dwell Brahmans or ascetics, or men of various denominations, or householders, upon whom is laid this duty of hearkening to superiors, hearkening to father and mother, hearkening to teachers, and proper treatment of friends, acquaintances, comrades, relatives, slaves, and servants, with fidelity of attachment. To such people in such a country befalls violence, or slaughter, or separation from their loved ones. Or misfortune befalls the friends, acquaintances, comrades, and relatives of those who are themselves well protected, while their affection is undiminished. Thus for them also that is a mode of violence. All these several happenings to men are matter of regret to His Sacred Majesty; because it is never the case that people have not faith in some one denomination or other.

Thus of all the people who were then slain, done to death, or carried away captive in the Kalingas, if the hundredth or the thousandth part were to suffer the same fate, it would now be matter of regret to His Sacred Majesty. Moreover, should any one do him wrong that too must be borne with by His Sacred Majesty, if it can possibly be borne with. Even upon the forest folk in his dominions His Sacred Majesty looks kindly and he seeks their conversion, for (if he did not) repentance would come upon

His Sacred Majesty. They are bidden to turn from evil ways that they be not chastised. For His Sacred Majesty desires that all animate beings should have security, self-control, peace of mind, and joyousness.

And this is the chiefest conquest in the opinion of His Sacred Majesty--the conquest by the Law of Piety--this it is that is won by His Sacred Majesty both in his own dominions and in all the neighbouring realms as far as six hundred leagues--where the Greek (Yona) King named Antiochus dwells, and north of that Antiochus to where dwell the four (4) kings severally named Ptolemy, Antigonus, Magas, and Alexander; and in the south the (realms of the) Cholas and Pāndyas, with Ceylon likewise--and here too, in the King's dominions, among the Yonas, and Kambojas, among the Nābhapaṃtis of Nābhaka, among the Bhojas and Pitinikas, among the Āndhras and Pulindas--everywhere men follow His Sacred Majesty's instruction in the Law of Piety. Even where the envoys of His Sacred Majesty do not penetrate, there too men hearing His Sacred Majesty's ordinance based on the Law of Piety and his instruction in that Law, practise and will practise the Law.

And, again, the conquest thereby won everywhere is everywhere a conquest full of delight. Delight is found in the conquests made by the Law. That delight, however, is only a small matter. His Sacred

Majesty regards as bearing much fruit only that which concerns the other world.
And for this purpose has this pious edict been written in order that my sons and grandsons, who may be, should not regard it as their duty to conquer a new conquest. If, perchance, they become engaged in a conquest by arms, they should take pleasure in patience and gentleness, and regard as (the only true) conquest the conquest won by piety. That avails for both this world and the next. Let all joy be in effort, because that avails for both this world and the next.'

ROCK EDICT XIV.
EPILOGUE.

'This set of edicts of the Law of Piety has been written by command of His Sacred and Gracious Majesty the King in a form sometimes condensed, sometimes of medium length, and sometimes expanded; because everything is not suitable in every place, for my dominions are extensive, and much has been written and much I shall cause to be written.
Certain phrases have been uttered again and again by reason of the honeyed sweetness of such and such a topic, in the hope that the people may act up to them. It may be that something has been written incompletely by reason of mutilation of the order, or misunderstanding of the sense, or a blunder of the engraver.'

THE KALINGA EDICTS.

I. THE BORDERERS' EDICT.

THE DUTIES OF OFFICIALS TO THE BORDER TRIBES.

'Thus saith His Sacred Majesty:--

At Samāpā the officers are to be addressed in the King's words as fōllows:--

Whatsoever my views are I desire them to be acted on in practice and carried into effect by certain means. And in my opinion the chief means fōr attaining this purpose are my instructions to you. ❧ "All men are my children"; and just as I desire fōr my children that they may enjoy every kind of prosperity and happiness in both this world and the next, so also I desire the same fōr all men.

If you ask, "With regard to the unsubdued borderers what is the King's command to us?" or "What truth it is that I desire the borderers to grasp?"--the answer is that the King desires that "they should not be afraid of me, that they should trust me, and should receive from me happiness, not sorrow." Moreover, they should grasp the truth that "the King will bear patiently with us, so fār as it is possible to bear with us," and that "for my sake they should follow the Law of Piety and so gain both this world and the next."

And for this purpose I give you instructions. In this way I am discharged of my debt when I have instructed you and intimated my will, my inflexible resolve and promise.

Now you, acting accordingly, must do your work, and must make these people trust me and grasp the truth that--"The King is to us even as a father; he loves us even as he loves himself; we are to the King even as his children."

By instructing you and intimating my will, my inflexible resolve and promise, I shall have (trained) local officials for this business, because you are in a position to make these people trust me and to ensure their prosperity and happiness in both this world and the next, and by so doing you can both win heaven and discharge your debt to me. And for this purpose has this edict been here inscribed in order that the officers may strive without ceasing to secure the trust of these borderers, and set them moving on the path of piety.

And this edict must be recited at the beginning of each Season of four months on the Tishya day, and, as occasion offers, it may be recited on a Tishya day in the intervals, even to a single hearer. Endeavour by acting thus to fulfil my behests.'

KALINGA EDICT II.

THE PROVINCIALS' EDICT.

THE DUTIES OF OFFICIALS TO THE PROVINCIALS.

'By command of His Sacred Majesty:--At Tosali the officers in charge of the town are to be addressed as follows:--

Whatsoever my views are I desire them to be acted on in practice and carried into effect by certain means. And in my opinion the chief means for attaining this purpose are my instructions to you, because you have been set over many thousands of living beings that you may gain the affection of good men.

"All men are my children," and just as I desire for my children that they may enjoy every kind of prosperity and happiness in both this world and the next, so also I desire the same for all men. You, however, do not grasp this truth to its full extent. Some individual, perchance, pays heed, but to a part only, not the whole. See then to this, for the principle is well established.

Again, it happens that some individual incurs imprisonment or other ill-usage, and (?) when that happens without due cause many other people are deeply grieved. In such a case you must desire to do justice.

However, with certain natural dispositions success is impossible, to wit, envy, lack of perseverance, harshness, impatience, want of application, laziness, indolence. You must desire that such dispositions be not yours. The root of the whole matter lies in perseverance and patience in applying the principle. The indolent man cannot rouse himself to move; but one must needs move, advance, go on.

In the same way you must see to your duty, and be told to remember:--"See to my commands; such and such are the instructions of His Sacred Majesty." Fulfilment of these bears great fruit, non-fulfilment brings great calamity. By those who fail neither heaven nor the royal favour can be won. Ill performance of this duty can never gain my regard, whereas in fulfilling my instructions you will win heaven and also pay your debt to me.

This edict must be recited every Tishya constellation day, and at intervals, on fit occasions, it may be recited even to a single hearer. By such actions you must endeavour to fulfil my behests.

For this purpose has this edict been here inscribed in order that the officers in charge of the town may strive without ceasing to prevent the imprisonment or ill-usage of the townsmen without due cause.

And for this purpose, in accordance with the Law of Piety, I shall send forth on circuit every five years such officers as are of mild and temperate disposition, regardful of the sanctity of life, who knowing this purpose will act in accordance with my instructions.

From Ujjain the Prince will send forth people of a similar class for the same purpose, but will not overpass the limit of three years.
The same order applies to Taxila.
When the officers aforesaid proceed on circuit, then without neglecting their own ordinary business, they will attend to this matter also and act in accordance with the King's instructions.'

THE SEVEN PILLAR EDICTS.

PILLAR EDICT I.

THE PRINCIPLES OF GOVERNMENT.

'Thus saith His Sacred and Gracious Majesty the King:--
When I had been consecrated twenty-six years I caused this pious edict to be written. Both this world and the next are hard to secure save by intense love of the Law of Piety, intense self-examination, intense obedience, intense dread, and intense effort. However, owing to my instructions, this yearning for and love of the Law of Piety from day to day have grown and will grow. My Agents, too, whether of high, low, or middle rank, themselves conform to my teaching, and lead in the right way--for fickle-minded people, must be led into the right way--and the wardens of the marches act in like manner.
For this is the rule--protection by the Law of Piety, regulation by that law, felicity by that law, and security by that law.'

PILLAR EDICT II.

THE ROYAL EXAMPLE.

'Thus saith His Sacred and Gracious Majesty the King:--

"The Law of Piety is excellent."

"But wherein consists the Law of Piety?"

"In these things, to wit, in abstinence from impiety, in many good deeds, compassion, liberality, truthfulness, and purity."

The gift of spiritual insight I have given in manifold ways; on two-footed and four-footed creatures, on birds, and the denizens of the waters, I have conferred various favours, even unto the boon of life, and many other good deeds have I done.

For this purpose I have caused this pious edict to be written, that men may walk after its teaching and that it may long endure; and he who will follow its teaching will do well.'

PILLAR EDICT III.

SELF-EXAMINATION.

'Thus saith His Sacred and Gracious Majesty the King:--

Man sees his every good deed, and says, "This good deed have I done." In no wise does he see his ill deed, and say, "This ill deed have I done, this act called impiety."

Difficult, verily, is this needful self-examination. Nevertheless, a man should see to this knowing that

these things lead to impiety, to wit, brutality, cruelty, anger, pride, jealousy--and should say, "By reason of these may I not fall."
This chiefly must be seen to--"The one course avails for this present world; the other course avails me also for the world to come."'

❀

PILLAR EDICT IV.

THE POWERS AND DUTIES OF COMMISSIONERS.

'Thus saith His Sacred and Gracious Majesty the King:--
After I had been consecrated twenty-six years I caused this pious edict to be written.
My Commissioners are set over many hundreds of thousands of the people--and I have granted to them independence in the award of honours and penalties in order that the Commissioners in security and fearlessness may perform their duties, bestow welfare and happiness on the people of the country, and confer benefits upon them. They will ascertain the causes of happiness and sorrow, and, through the (subordinate) officials of the Law of Piety, will exhort the people of the country so that they may gain both this world and the next.
For the Commissioners are eager to obey me, while my Agents will obey my will and orders, and they too will, on occasion, give exhortations whereby the

Commissioners may be zealous to win my favour. For, just as a man having made over a child to a skilful nurse feels secure, and says to himself, "The skilful nurse is zealous to care for my child's happiness," even so my Commissioners have been appointed for the welfare and happiness of the country people, with intent that they in fearlessness, security, and quietness may perform their duties, and for that reason my Commissioners have been granted independence in the award of honours and penalties.

Forasmuch as it is desirable that there should be uniformity in judicial proceedings and uniformity in penalties, from this time forward my rule is this:--"To condemned men lying in prison under sentence of death a respite of three days is granted by me." During that interval the relatives of some of the condemned will invite them to deep meditation, hoping to save their lives, or will themselves present offerings and undergo fasts with a view to the other world in order to promote the pious meditations of those about to die.

For my desire is that, even in the time of their confinement, the condemned men may gain the next world, and that among the people pious practices of various kinds may grow, including self-control and distribution of alms.'

PILLAR EDICT V.

REGULATIONS RESTRICTING SLAUGHTER AND MUTILATION OF ANIMALS.

'Thus saith His Sacred and Gracious Majesty the King:—

After I had been consecrated twenty-six years the following species were declared exempt from slaughter, to wit:—

Parrots, starlings, (?) adjutants, "Brahmani ducks," geese, nandīmukhas, gelātas, bats, queen-ants, female tortoises, "boneless fish," vedaveyakas, gangāpupuṭakas, (?) skate, (? river) tortoises, porcupines, tree-squirrels, (?) bārasingha deer, "Brahmani bulls," (?) monkeys, rhinoceros, grey doves, village pigeons, and all four-footed animals which are not utilized or eaten.

She-goats, ewes, and sows, that is to say, those either with young or in milk, are exempt from slaughter, as well as their offspring up to six months of age.

The caponing of cocks must not be done.

Chaff must not be burned along with the living things in it.

Forests must not be burned, either for mischief or so as to destroy life.

The living must not be fed with the living.

At each of the three seasonal full moons, and at the full moon of the month Tishya (December-January), for three days in each case, namely, the fourteenth and fifteenth of the first fortnight, and the opening day of the second fortnight, as well as on the fast-days throughout the year, fish is exempt from killing and may not be sold.

On the same days, in elephant-preserves and fish-ponds no other classes of animals may be destroyed.

On the eighth, fourteenth, and fifteenth days of each fortnight, as well as on the Tishya and Punarvasu days, on the three seasonal full-moon days and on festival days bulls must not be castrated, and he-goats, rams, boars, or other animals which are commonly castrated must not be castrated.

On the Tishya and Punarvasu days, on the seasonal full-moon days, and during the seasonal full-moon fortnights, the branding of horses and oxen must not be done.

Up to the date that I had been consecrated for twenty-six years--in that interval the release of prisoners has been effected by me twenty-five times.'

PILLAR EDICT VI.

THE NECESSITY FOR A DEFINITE CREED.

'Thus saith His Sacred and Gracious Majesty the King:--

After I had been consecrated twelve years I caused pious edicts to be written for the welfare and happiness of mankind, with the intent that they, giving up their old courses, might attain growth in piety, one way or another. Thus, aiming at the welfare and

happiness of mankind, with that object I devote my attention alike to my relatives, to persons near, and to persons afăr off, if haply I may guide some of them to happiness; and thus I make my arrangements. In like manner I devote my attention to all communities. For all denominations are reverenced by me with various forms of reverence. Nevertheless, this personal adherence to one's own creed, is the chief thing in my opinion.
After I had been consecrated twenty-six years I caused this pious edict to be written.'

PILLAR EDICT VII.

REVIEW OF THE KING'S MEASURES FOR THE PROPAGATION OF THE LAW OF PIETY.

I. 'Thus saith His Sacred and Gracious Majesty the King:
The Kings who lived in times past desired that men might grow with the growth of the Law of Piety. Men, however, did not grow with the growth of the Law of Piety in due proportion.
II. Then thus said His Sacred and Gracious Majesty the King:--This thought occurred to me:--The Kings who lived in times past desired that men might in due proportion grow with the growth of the Law of Piety. Men, however, did not grow with the growth of the Law of Piety in due proportion. By what means then can men be induced to con-

form? By what means can men grow with the growth of the Law of Piety in due proportion? By what means can I lift up at least some of them so as to grow with the growth of Piety?

III. Then thus said His Sacred and Gracious Majesty the King:--This thought occurred to me:--I will cause the precepts of the Law of Piety to be preached, and with instructions in that Law will I instruct, so that men hearkening unto them may conform thereto, lift themselves up, and vigorously grow with the growth of Piety.

For this my purpose the precepts of that Law have been preached, instructions in that Law of many kinds have been disseminated, so that my Agents set over the multitude may expound and expand my teaching.

The Commissioners, too, set over many hundred thousands of souls, have received instructions from me--"In such and such a manner expound my teaching to the subordinate officials of the Law of Piety."

IV. Thus saith His Sacred and Gracious Majesty:--Considering further the same purpose, I have set up pillars of the Law, appointed Censors of the Law, and composed precepts of the Law.

V. Thus saith His Sacred and Gracious Majesty the King:--

On the roads I have had banyan trees planted to give shade to man and beast; I have had groves of mango-trees planted; at every half-kōs I have had wells dug; rest-houses have been erected; and numerous watering places have been provided by me here and there for the enjoyment of man and beast. A small matter, however, is that so-called enjoyment. With various blessings has mankind been blessed by former Kings as by me. In my case, however, with the intent that men may conform to the Law of Piety, as my thought was, so has it been done.

VI. Thus saith His Sacred and Gracious Majesty:--
My Censors of the Law of Piety, too, are occupied with many objects of the (royal) favour, affecting both ascetics and householders, and are likewise occupied with all denominations. I have arranged, also, that they should be occupied with the affairs of the Buddhist clergy, as well as among the Brahmans and Ājīvikas, the Jains, and, in fact, various denominations. The several ordinary officials shall severally superintend their respective charges, whereas the Censors of the Law of Piety shall superintend all other denominations in addition to such special charges.

VII. Thus saith His Sacred and Gracious Majesty the King:--
These and many other high officers are employed in the distribution of the royal alms, both my own and those of the Queens; and in all my households, these officers, both here (at the capital) and in the provinces, in divers ways indicate the manifold opportunities for charity (?). I have also arranged

that the same officers should be employed in the distribution of the alms of my sons and of the princes, the Queens' sons, for the promotion of pious acts and conformity to the Law of Piety. For the pious acts and conformity referred to are those whereby compassion, liberality, truth, purity, gentleness, and saintliness will thus grow among mankind.

VIII. Thus saith His Sacred and Gracious Majesty the King:--

Whatsoever meritorious deeds I have done, those deeds the people have conformed to and will imitate, whence the result follows that they have grown and will grow in the virtues of hearkening to father and mother, hearkening to teachers, reverence for the aged, and seemly treatment of Brahmans and ascetics, of the poor and wretched, yea, even of slaves and servants.

IX. Thus saith His Sacred and Gracious Majesty the King:--

Among men wherever the aforesaid growth of piety has developed, it has been effected by two-fold means, to wit, pious regulations and meditation. Of these two means, however, pious regulations are of small account, whereas meditation is superior.

Nevertheless, pious regulations have been issued by me to the effect that such and such species are exempt from slaughter, and there are many other pious regulations which I have issued. But the superior effect of meditation is seen in the growth of piety among men, and the more complete abstention from the killing of animate beings and from the sacrifice of living creatures.

For this purpose has this (edict) been issued, that, so long as the sun and moon endure, my sons and descendants may conform thereto, for by such conformity the gain of both this world and the next is assured.

After I had been consecrated twenty-seven years I caused this pious edict to be written.

X. Concerning this His Sacred Majesty saith:--This pious edict, wheresoever pillars of stone or tables of stone exist, must be inscribed, so that it may long endure.'

THE MINOR PILLAR EDICTS.

I. THE SĀRNĀTH PILLAR EDICT.

THE PENALTY OF SCHISM.

'Thus saith His Sacred Majesty:-- . . . .

[At] Pāṭa[liputra (?) and in the provinces His Majesty's commands are that] the Church may not be rent in twain by any person. But whosoever, monk or nun, shall break the unity of the Church shall be compelled to wear white garments and to dwell in a place not reserved for the clergy.

Thus this ordinance must be published in the congregation of monks and in the congregation of nuns.

Thus saith His Sacred Majesty:--

One copy of this edict has been posted for your use in your (?) office, and one similar copy of it you must post up for the information of the laity, so that the lay people may attend on each fāst-day to make themselves fāmiliar with this ordinance; and on the fāst-days throughout the year every official should attend the fāst-day service to make himself fāmiliar and acquainted with this ordinance.
And so fār as your jurisdiction extends you must send it out everywhere according to this text, and likewise in garrisons and the Districts you must cause it to be sent out according to this text.'

MINOR PILLAR EDICT II.

THE KAUŚĀMBĪ EDICT.

The same Subject.

'His Sacred Majesty instructs the officials of Kausāmbī as follows . . . .
The Way of the Church must not be quitted. . . .
Whosoever shall break the unity of the Church, whether monk or nun from this time forth, shall be compelled to wear white garments, and to dwell in a place not reserved for the clergy.'

MINOR PILLAR EDICT III.

THE SĀNCHĪ PILLAR EDICT.

The same subject.

. . . . The Way [of the Church] has been made . . . . Whosoever shall break the unity of the Church, whether monk or nun, shall be compelled to wear white garments and to dwell in a place not reserved for the clergy.
For my desire is that the Way of the Church may long endure.'

MINOR PILLAR EDICT IV.

THE QUEEN'S EDICT.

THE DONATIONS OF THE SECOND QUEEN.

'By command of His Sacred Majesty the officials everywhere are to be addressed as follows:—
Whatever donation has been made by the Second Queen, be it a mango-grove, pleasure-garden, charitable hostel, or aught else, is to be accounted as the act of that Queen. All transactions of the kind are [? for the acquisition of merit by] the Second Queen, the Kāruvāki, mother of Tīvara.'

MISCELLANEOUS INSCRIPTIONS.

THE COMMEMORATIVE TARĀI PILLAR INSCRIPTIONS.

I. THE RUMMINDĒĪ INSCRIPTION.

COMMEMORATION OF ASOKA'S VISIT TO THE BIRTHPLACE OF BUDDHA SAKYAMUNI.

'His Sacred and Gracious Majesty the King, when he had been consecrated twenty years, having come in person did reverence, and because "Here Buddha was born, the Sakya sage" (?) a great stone railing was prepared and a stone pillar was erected.

Because "Here the Venerable One was born" the village of Lummini was made free of (religious) cesses and declared entitled to the eighth share (of the produce due to the Crown).'

TARĀI PILLAR II.

THE NIGLĪVA PILLAR.

COMMEMORATION OF ASOKA'S VISIT TO THE STŪPA OF KONĀKAMANA BUDDHA.

'His Sacred and Gracious Majesty the King, when he had been consecrated fourteen years, enlarged for the second time the stūpa of Buddha Konākamana; and (when he had been consecrated twenty years), coming in person, did reverence and erected (a stone pillar).'

THE BARĀBAR CAVE DEDICATIONS OF ASOKA.

BESTOWAL OF CAVE-DWELLINGS ON THE ĀJĪVIKAS.

I. THE SUDĀMA OR BANYAN-TREE CAVE.

'This "banyan-tree" cave was granted to the Ājīvikas by the King's Grace when he had been consecrated twelve years.'

II. THE VISVA-JHOPRI OR KHALATIKA HILL CAVE.

'This cave in the Khalatika hill was granted to the Ājīvikas by the King's Grace when he had been consecrated twelve years.'

III. THE KARNA-CHAUPAR OR SUPIYĀ CAVE.

'The King's Grace when consecrated nineteen years granted (?) the Supiyā cave in the (?) Khalatika hill for as long as sun and moon endure.'

THE NĀGĀRJUNI CAVE DEDICATIONS OF DAŚARATHA.

BESTOWAL OF CAVE-DWELLINGS ON THE ĀJĪVIKAS.

I. THE VAHIYAKĀ CAVE.

'The Vahiyakā Cave was assigned by Dasaratha, His Sacred Majesty, immediately after his accession, to the venerable Ājīvikas as a dwelling-place, for as long as the sun and moon endure.'

II. THE GOPIKĀ CAVE.

Identical with I., except for the name of the cave.

III. THE VADATHIKĀ CAVE.

Identical with I. and II., except for the name of the cave.

COMMENTARY.

MINOR ROCK EDICT I.

This remarkable edict has been found in six places. Three copies of it exist on rocks at or near Siddāpura in northern Mysore, of which the one on the Brahmagiri hill is practically perfect. The two copies in the neighbourhood are badly damaged but seem to be identical with the Brahmagiri text. The recensions found at Rūpnāth in the Central Provinces, Sahasrām in the Shāhābad District of South Bihār, and at Bairāt in Rājputāna differ in some details from each other and from the Siddāpura copies. It has been therefore thought necessary to translate both the Brahmagiri text, the best preserved of the Mysore copies, and the Rūpnāth recension, the most perfect of the northern copies.

The three northern recensions of the first edict are not directed to any particular persons, but, like most of the edicts, were intended for general information. The Siddāpura copies are addressed specially to the officials of an unknown town named Isila by order of the Prince and officials at Suvarṇagiri.

The document has been the subject of much learned discussion, and general agreement as to its interpretation has not yet been attained. The phrase 'more than two years and a half' should be read according to some scholars as either 'thirty-two years and a half' or as 'thirty-eight years and a half.' Similarly, the phrases 'more than a year' and 'one year, in fact, more than a year' are sometimes converted into 'a period of six years or rather more than six years.' The mysterious concluding sentence is a puzzle difficult to solve. The varying views concerning the meaning of this edict involve widely divergent opinions on the history of Asoka.

It is impossible in this place to enter into the controversy, and it will suffice to say that the translator now agrees with M. Senart and Mr. F. W. Thomas that the renderings 'more than two years and a half,' and 'one year, in fact, more than a year' are correct, and is satisfied that the figures 256 (repeated in words at Sahasrām) are not a date. He further accepts the view of Mr. F. W. Thomas that the word *Vyutha*, with its variants, refers to Asoka, and not to Buddha, or any one else. Asoka, in his 11th 'regnal year' (259 B.C.), 'went forth on the road to wisdom (*sambodhi*)' and organized 'pious tours' (Rock Edict VIII.), and, as this document informs us, at the same time began to exert himself strenuously. In the course of 'more than a year,' say some sixteen months, he moved about with such zealous rapidity that he changed his camp or temporary abode 256 times, and so made 256 *vivāsas*. As the person who performed this feat he dubbed himself Vyutha, the man on the move, or the 'Traveller.'. The final words seem to designate him also as the Sata, of which the meaning is doubtful. It may be noted that $256 = 16^2 = 64 \times 4 = 32 \times 8$, and that all these numbers are much fancied by Hindus, so that 256 may be regarded as a 'perfect number.'

The main purpose of the edict is to enforce the brief precept (*sāvane*), 'Let small and great exert themselves,' which, according to the Rūpnath version, was 'made' or 'composed' by the Vyutha, and, according to the Brahmagiri text, was 'proclaimed' by him. We are informed by sections 3 and 4 of Pillar Edict VII. that Asoka both 'proclaimed' or 'caused to be preached' and 'made' or 'composed' (*kaṭe*) the precepts (*sāvane*) of the Law. The attribution in this edict of the same actions in the same terms to the Vyutha goes a long way to prove that that term refers to Asoka himself.

The Prince at Suvarṇagiri appears to mean the Viceroy of the South. The theory that the phrase designates the Prince Regent residing at Songiri, one of the hills at Rājagṛiha, the ancient capital of Magadha, and supposed to be administering the empire after Asoka's assumed abdication, does not seem to me to rest on any solid foundation; nor can I find sufficient reason for believing that Asoka abdicated at all.

As regards the date of the edict, M. Senart and Mr. F. W. Thomas hold it to be the earliest of the whole collection, and place it in the beginning of the 13th 'regnal year.' The fact that this document speaks of edicts to be issued in the future only, without reference to any preceding, is, as M. Senart observes, strong evidence in favour of its priority. We know from the testimony of Pillar Edict VI. that Asoka began the practice of issuing 'pious edicts' in that 13th year, during the course of which Rock Edicts III. and IV. were prepared. Dr. Fleet, on the contrary, believes the Minor Rock edicts to be the latest of all. The translator, after much consideration, is convinced that M. Senart and Mr. Thomas are right.

A few separate phrases require explanation.

A great man.—Such as Asoka.

One-and-a-half fold.—Used in an indefinite sense to mean 'in great measure.'

Send it out.—The verb is the causal of *vivas*, and the meaning is settled by the corresponding passage in the Sārnāth Pillar Edict, where M. Boyer translates the word by '*envoyez.*'

Stone pillar.—No copy of this edict on a pillar has been discovered.

THE SAME EDICT (BRAHMAGIRI TEXT).

See comment on the Rūpnāth text.

All over India—literally 'in Jambudvīpa,' one of the seven mythological continents, including India and something more.

The men regarded as gods seem to be the Brahmans. Compare Sherring's description of the Brahman of Benares:—"With the idea constantly before his inner self that he is himself a god and deserves divine honours—which is not a mere freak of a deluded imagination on his part, but is acknowledged by all Hindus, some of whom as he pursues his way will stop him and then offer to him the adoration due only to the Almighty, which he receives as his right" (*The Sacred City of the Hindus, p.* 14). The Rūpnāth version commemorates the dethronement of the Hindu gods themselves. This edict expresses the hot zeal of the new convert, strenuously exerting himself. The later documents breathe a spirit of wide toleration.

MINOR ROCK EDICT II.

This short edict is appended to Edict I. in all the three Mysore recensions, but is not found at Rūpnāth, Sahasrām, or Bairāt. It differs in style from the numerous similar summaries in the Rock and Pillar Edicts, and looks as if it had been drawn up in the office of the Viceroy of the South. The scribe's signature is partly written in the Kharoshṭhī character used on the north-western frontier. The writer evidently was an official imported from the north, who wished to show off his knowledge of both alphabets. The words 'written by Paḍa' are in the Brahmī character of the text, while the words 'the scribe' are in Kharoshṭhī read from right to left. The Brahmagiri text, which is perfect, has been translated.

THE BHĀBRĀ EDICT.

The very ancient small town of Bairāt (27° 27′ N., 76° 12′ E.) is situated in the Jaypur State, Rājputāna, about forty-two miles N.N.E. of Jaypur and a hundred miles almost due west of Mathurā. The summit of a hill to the south-west of the town is crowned by the ruins of a *stūpa* and two Buddhist monasteries. The inscription now known as the Bhābrā Edict is incised on a granite boulder, which formerly lay upon the lower platform of one of those monasteries, but was removed many years ago to the rooms of the Asiatic Society of Bengal at Calcutta. Considering the purport and mode of publication of the edict it is reasonable to suppose that it was issued by Asoka when residing in one of the monasteries on the hill. A copy of the First Minor Rock Edict is incised on the south face of a great cubical block of granite at the foot of the Pāṇdus' Hill also close to the town. It is possible, or even probable, that the two inscriptions may be strictly contemporary, but neither presents any clear internal evidence of date. Both are so important for the history of both Buddhism and Asoka that the difficulty in dating them exactly is unfortunate.

The Minor Rock Edicts have been discussed in the comment on those documents, and need not be referred to further here. The Bhābrā Edict, like that on the Sārnāth Pillar, is addressed officially by the emperor as Head of the Church to the Buddhist Clergy, Church, Order, or Congregation of monks and nuns (*saṅgha*). He calls himself simply *Piyadasi lājā Māgadhe*, which may be rendered, in Tudor style, as 'His Grace the King (or 'The King's Grace') of Magadha.' Dr. Bloch informs me that the adjective undoubtedly is in the nominative case, and must be construed with *lājā* (=*Rājā*), and not with *saṅgham*. Asoka does not describe himself as 'King of Magadha' (S. Bihār) in any other document.

The purpose of the edict is to recommend to all faithful Buddhists, clerical and lay, male and female, the study of seven passages or texts of Buddha's teaching, special favourites of His Majesty. The names of the seven texts are set out in the dialect of Magadha, and five of them, Nos. 2, 3, 4, 5, and 7 have been identified with certainty in the Nikāya portion of the Pāli scriptures. Of these one only, No. 3, entitled 'Fears of What may Happen,' has been translated. It enumerates the physical and moral dangers to which recluses are exposed, and offers little of interest to the modern reader. But to the intensely practical mind of Asoka it seems to have appeared valuable as a handy guide to the ascetic life. M. Senart has printed the text of No. 7, 'The Address to Rāhula,' without a translation. That tract is labelled as the one 'beginning with the subject of Falsehood' in order to distinguish it from other Addresses to Rāhula which exist in the Canon. The text of the one favoured by Asoka occupies five closely printed large pages. M. Sylvain Lévi has translated a Chinese recension.

It seems to me difficult to resist the inference from these facts that the Nikāya portion of the Canon existed written in the Magadhī tongue in Asoka's days, but in 1886 M. Senart was of opinion that the Buddhism of that age was '*dépourvue encore de textes fixés par l' écriture et à coup sûr d' un canon régulièrement défini.*' Possibly the learned author might take a different view now.

In addition to the seven longer passages recommended for study Asoka quotes as his special favourite the short text: 'Thus the Good Law will long endure,' which is found in both the *Mahāvuytpatti* and the *Anguttara Nikāya* of the Pāli Canon. His intense desire to fulfil the promise of that text was the motive which induced him to record the principles of the Good Law on imperishable tables and pillars of stone engraved with the most scrupulous care and exquisite skill, regardless of cost.

The preamble of the edict proves that Asoka was familiar with the well-known formula of the 'Three Refuges' or 'Three Jewels,' which recurs so often in the Canon, and is most forcibly expressed in the Ordination Service as still used in Ceylon:—

> 'I put my trust in Buddha.
> I put my trust in the Law.
> I put my trust in the priesthood.
> Again I put my trust in Buddha.
> Again I put my trust in the Law.
> Again I put my trust in the priesthood.
> Once more I put my trust in Buddha.
> Once more I put my trust in the Law.
> Once more I put my trust in the priesthood' (Warren, *Buddhism in Translations*, p. 396).

The Buddhism of the Bhābrā Edict and the Minor Pillar Edicts evidently was an institution highly organized, and personally I feel assured that its principles had been reduced to writing in a form not differing widely from the Nikāya portion of the Pāli Canon. The title of the first passage recommended by Asoka, 'The Exaltation of Vinaya,' which has not yet been identified with certainty, proves that treatises on *vinaya*, or monastic discipline, also were extant, while the Minor Pillar Edicts bear witness to the strictness with which Asoka in his double capacity as Emperor and as Head of the Church or Defender of the Faith enforced disciplinary rules on monks and nuns. One other point may be noticed—the apparent importance of the nuns in those times. Perhaps it is hardly necessary to remark that in this edict *dhaṃma* means the body of Buddha's doctrine, and has not the more purely ethical sense that it has in the other edicts.

ROCK EDICT I.

His Sacred and Gracious Majesty the King.—The Girnār text reads *devānaṃpriyo priyadasi rājā.* The first word, meaning etymologically 'dear to the Gods' (*devas*), was used by various kings as a royal title, and is better treated as the equivalent of the old English Stuart title 'His Sacred Majesty' than by etymological analysis. So the title or epithet *piyadasi* (*priyadarśin*), which literally means 'of gracious look,' or the like, should not be regarded as a personal name, but should be rendered, in connexion with *rājā*, as 'His Gracious Majesty the King,' or by some similar formal phrase. Thus the complete royal style of Asoka, ceremoniously thrice repeated in full in this first edict, may be appropriately represented by the phrase 'His Sacred and Gracious Majesty the King.' Asoka never uses his personal name in the inscriptions.

Here (in the capital).—The interpretation of 'here' is suggested by Rock Edict V. in which the Girnār text inserts 'at Pāṭaliputra' to explain the word 'here' used by itself in the other versions.

Holiday-feasts.—'Festive assemblies' (Bühler). The *samāja* was a merry meeting, generally held on the top of a hill, at which feasting on meat and liquor was accompanied by dancing, singing, music, recitations, conjuring tricks, and acrobatic shows. Mr. Bhandarkar interprets the words 'are (*asti*) meritorious' in the sense of 'used to be.' But perhaps the contrast is between 'the capital' and 'certain places' (*ekachā*).

Many hundred thousands.—'Many thousands' in Kālsī version.

ROCK EDICT II.

Cholas.—According to tradition the Chola country (*Choḷamaṇḍaıam*) was bounded on the north by the Pennār, and on the south by the southern Vellāru river; or, in other words, it extended along the eastern coast from Nellore to Pudukottai, where it abutted on the Pāṇḍya territory. On the west it reached to the borders of Coorg. The limits thus defined include Madras, and several other British districts on the east, as well as the greater part of the Mysore state. The most ancient capital was Uṛaiyūr, or Old Trichinopoly, so far as is known with certainty. The Pennār river probably was the northern Chola frontier in the time of Asoka.

Pāndyas.—The Pāṇḍya kingdom occupied the plain country of the Madura and Tinnevelly Districts, and sometimes comprised the southern section of Travancore, known as Ven. The most ancient capital was Korkai or Kolkai on the Tāmraparṇī river, a great port until it was silted up and superseded by Kāyal, three miles lower down. In the time of Pliny (77 A.D.) the capital was Madura.

Satiyaputra.—The kingdom of Satiyaputra is mentioned in this inscription only, and is supposed to be the Tuluva country, of which Mangalore is the centre. The Chandragiri river in the South Kanara District forms the boundary between Tuluva, where the Tulu language is spoken, and Malabar, or Kerala, where the language is Malayālam.

Ketalaputra.—In other versions *Keralaputra*, that is to say, Malabar, to the south of the Chandragiri river, extending to Cape Comorin, and including the present Malabar District, with the Travancore and Cochin States. It is also known as the Chera Kingdom, and sometimes comprised the Kongu region, corresponding to the modern Coimbatore District with the southern part of Salem. The earliest capital was Vanji (Vanchi or Karūr), about 28 miles E.N.E. of Cochin.

Tradition uniformly states the kingdoms of Tamilakam, or Tamil Land, to be three, namely, the Pāṇḍya, Chera or Kerala, and Chola. Asoka adds Satiyaputra, which probably was generally included in Kerala.

Ceylon.—*Tambapaṃni* (*Tāmraparṇī*), the 'utmost Indian isle Taprobane' of Milton.

Antiochus, the Greek King.—Antiochus Theos, King of Syria and western Asia, who died in 247 or 246 B.C. He was son of Antiochus Soter and grandson of Seleucus Nicator, the opponent, and afterwards the ally of Asoka's grandfather, Chandragupta Maurya.

The Kings near unto that Antiochus.—Enumerated in Rock Edict XIII. in the words 'even to where the Greek (*Yona*) King named Antiochus dwells, and north of (or 'beyond') that Antiochus to where dwell the four Kings severally named Ptolemy, Antigonus, Magas, and Alexander;' for identification of whom see commentary on Rock Edict XIII.

Curative arrangements.—The word is *chikīchha*, rendered by Kern 'the system of caring for the sick;' by Senart 'remedies,' by Bühler 'hospitals,' and by Bhandarkar 'provisions' or 'provident arrangement.'

Wells have been dug and trees planted.—Compare Pillar Edict VII.:—'On the roads I have had banyan-trees planted to give shade to man and beast; I have had groves of mango-trees planted; at every half-*kos* ('at intervals of eight *kos*,' Fleet) I have had wells dug; rest-houses have been erected; and numerous watering-places have been provided by me here and there for the enjoyment of man and beast.'

ROCK EDICT III.

The interpretation of this edict has given occasion to much difference of opinion, but there is now no doubt that *anusaṃyāna* means 'tour of inspection,' or 'circuit,' not 'general assembly,' as it was formerly rendered. The purpose of the command is to impose on all grades of officials during their quinquennial circuits through their jurisdictions a special extra duty, namely, the proclamation of the Law of Piety (*dharma*), as defined by His Majesty. The concluding sentence is a supplementary order enjoining the checking of stores and accounts, apparently those belonging to monastic bodies.

Consecrated twelve years.—The main act in an Indian King's consecration, the ritual equivalent to coronation, was the ceremonial sprinkling or aspersion (*abhisheka*) by which he was dedicated to his office. Asoka did not undergo this ceremony until four years after his accession, possibly on account of disputes with rival claimants to the throne. He counted his regnal years from his *abhisheka*, not from his accession.

[*Subordinate*] *officials.*—The word *yuta* is taken as equivalent to *āyukta*, 'officials' of a subordinate kind, like police officers, as distinguished from the Commissioners and District Officers of higher rank. Others translate 'lieges' or 'the faithful.'

Commissioners and District Officers.—These modern official Anglo-Indian designations are used as rough equivalents of *rājūke* and *prādesike.*

Law of Piety.—The Hindu *dharma*, or rule of a good man's life, with the special sense given to it by Asoka as defined in this edict. The Second Minor Rock Edict varies the formula. Other variants will be found in Rock Edicts IV., IX., XI., and Pillar Edict VII.

Other Duties.—General administrative and judicial work. Asoka imposes on his officers the additional burden of proclaiming his notion of *dharma.*

To spend little and store little.—This apparently correct interpretation of *apavyayatā apabhāṃdatā* is due to Mr. F. W. Thomas.

[*Monastic*] *communities.*—The local *saṃghas*, or monastic communities (Senart and F. W. Thomas). The word *parisā* (*parishad*) recurs in Rock Edict VI. The five *parishads*, according to Buddhist reckoning, were (1) *Bhikshus*, monks; (2) *Bhikshunis*, nuns; (3) *Sikshamānās*, female pupils; (4) *Sramaneras*, male novices; and (5) *Sramanerīs*, female novices. Sometimes (6) *Upāsakas* and (7) *Upāsikās*, male and female lay folk, are added, making 7 *Parishads* in all (Takakusu). Others reckon only 4 *Parishads*, Nos. 1, 2, 6, and 7 of the list above. Asoka probably referred to either the four or the five *parishads*. (See the Sārnāth Pillar Edict).

The reckoning with regard to both the objects and accounts.—The regulation seems to be intended to enforce by official supervision the monastic obligation to abstain from lavish expenditure or the accumulation of stores. In later ages many monastic communities became, as I-tsing remarks, 'very avaricious.' 'It is unseemly,' he says, 'for a monastery to have great wealth, granaries full of rotten corn, many servants, male and female, money and treasures hoarded in the treasury, without using any of these things, while all the members are suffering from poverty.' Asoka's regulation seems to be directed against such abuses.

ROCK EDICT IV.

This edict is one of several summaries of the imperial teaching on the subject of *Dharma*, viewed from a Buddhist standpoint. The progress of the practice of *Dharma* is likened to the reverberation of a war-drum, which is displaced by the drum of piety.

Heavenly spectacles.—The meaning of the passage is best illustrated by the description given by Fa-hien, the Chinese pilgrim at the beginning of the fifth century, of what he saw at Pāṭaliputra. He tells how the people there celebrated a procession of images in the second month of each year, with a score of four-wheeled cars, each five storeys high, but all differing in detail. 'On the day mentioned, the monks and laity within the borders all come together; they have singers and skilful musicians; they pay their devotions with flowers and incense. The Brahmans come and invite the Buddhas to enter the city. These do so in order, and remain two nights in it. All through the night, they keep lamps burning, have skilful music, and present offerings.'

Sons, etc.—This shows that Asoka had several sons.

The best of all deeds.—Compare Rock Edict XI.

ROCK EDICT V.

Now by me many good deeds have been done.—Compare Pillar Edict II., 'many other good deeds have I done.' The Buddhist is directed to work out his own salvation, and to rely on the accumulated merit of his good works. Thus, in Burma at the present day, 'when the man is dying, no monks will come, truly; but an old man, an old friend, father, perhaps, or an elder of the village, and he will talk to the dying man. He will say, "Think of your good deeds; think of all you have done well in this life. Think of your good deeds." . . . "Nothing," he said, "was so calming to a man's soul as to think of even one deed he had done well in his life"' (*The Soul of a People*).

Censors.—In later ages similar officers have been employed by Hindu governments in Kashmīr and other States to enforce the rules of *dharma.*

Yonas, etc.—The Yonas (Yavanas, Ionians) primarily meant the Greeks, but the term was used vaguely for the foreign populations on the north-western frontier. In Rock Edicts II. and XIII. Antiochus and the other Hellenistic Kings are called Yonas. Kāmbojas are supposed to be Tibetans. The Gāndhāras were the inhabitants of Gandhāra, the country around Peshāwar. The Rāshṭrikas probably mean the dwellers in the hills of the Western Ghāts, Mahārāshṭra. The Pitenikas were the people of Paithan on the upper Godāvarī. The Yonas, Kāmbojas, and Pitenikas are mentioned again in Rock Edict XIII.

Servants and masters.—'*Diener und Herren*' (R. O. Franke).
Here, at Pāṭaliputra.—The gloss, 'at Pāṭaliputra,' occurs only in the Girnār text, and serves to explain the word 'here' in Rock Edict I.
Devoted to piety, etc.—Senart's interpretation. But on reconsideration, I prefer to translate *dhaṃma yutasi* as 'subordinate officials of the Law.'

ROCK EDICT VI.

Except for certain words, the exact meaning of which is not known, this edict is easy to interpret, and the general sense is certain.
Bedroom, etc.—The meaning of some of these words is open to doubt.
Official reporters.—These are the overseers, or *episkopoi*, described by Megasthenes, to whom was 'assigned the duty of watching all that goes on, and making reports secretly to the king.' Similar officials, *akhbār-navīs*, often have been employed in recent times by native governments, which usually distrust the responsible officials.
Communities.—The same word, *parisā*, is used as in Rock Edict III., and should be interpreted as explained in the commentary on that document.
At any hour and at any place.—The accessibility on which Asoka prides himself, although not really conducive to the orderly dispatch of business, is extremely popular in India, where no qualification in a ruler is more valued than his readiness to listen to grievances anywhere and everywhere.
The utmost exertion.—Compare the precept in the first Minor Rock Edict, 'Let small and great exert themselves;' and many passages in the Buddhist scriptures, as for instance:—'Idleness is a disgrace; constant sloth is defilement. By strenuous striving and with the help of insight you should pull out the poisoned arrow of indolence' (*Utthana Sutta*).

ROCK EDICT VII.

For Asoka's attitude towards all denominations or sects (*pāshaṇḍa*), compare Rock Edicts XII., XIII. The steadfastness, or 'firm attachment' here recommended is the 'attachment' (*bhakti*) to one's own denomination spoken of in Rock Edict XII. The general idea of this edict is that although, owing to human frailty, no denomination attains perfection, nevertheless, all denominations have high aims, and deserve toleration. Everybody can do something to fulfil the law, and even partial fulfilment is better than nothing.

ROCK EDICT VIII.

The use of 'Kings' (*rājāno*) in the Girnār text of the preamble as the equivalent of *devānampiya* of other texts proves that the latter title should not be translated etymologically.

Hunting.—Megasthenes describes how Asoka's grandfather, Chandragupta Maurya, used to go to the chase 'in Bacchanalian fashion. Crowds of women surround him, and outside of this circle spearmen are ranged. The road is marked off with ropes, and it is death to approach the women. Men with drums and gongs lead the procession. The King hunts in the enclosure and shoots arrows from a platform, etc.' In later ages, when Buddhism had passed away, Indian sovereigns continued to make most elaborate arrangements to secure the pleasures of the chase. The regulations of Pillar Edict V., issued when Asoka had been consecrated twenty-six years, were designed to put strict limitations on hunting throughout the empire. No devout Buddhist can possibly take part in the chase.

Went forth on the road to wisdom (*ayāya sambodhim*).—The word *sambodhi* is a technical Buddhist term, meaning the wisdom, insight, or intelligence of the Arhat or saint, which is analyzed into seven constituents, namely, self-possession, investigation into the truth, energy, calm, joy, concentration, and magnanimity (Rhys Davids).

Visiting (*darśana*).—The term, still in common use, means the respectful visit to and viewing of an object or person deserving of veneration, which is an act of merit. The Tarāi Pillar Inscriptions (*post*) are records of a 'pious tour' actually performed by Asoka in his twenty-first regnal year.

Discussion.—Many Indian kings, Harsha, Akbar, and others, have loved disputations on questions of religion. Asoka, no doubt, when on tour collected multitudes of holy men such as now gather together on certain occasions. 'At the vast assemblies of *sādhus*, which occur once in every twelve years at Hardwār, at Nāsik, and at Allahabad, there are fixed halls of learned disputation, where, for hundreds of years, Hindu philosophy has been discussed, determined, and expanded, something in the fashion of the Welsh Eisteddfod. Here come the wandering monks from every part of India. Here the householder finds himself in vigorous and renewed relation to his faith. Here fresh voices of learning and devotion are able to win for themselves ecclesiastical authority' (Noble, *Web of Indian Life*).

ROCK EDICT IX.

The texts vary considerably in details, without affecting the general sense, which is clear. The translation is from Kālsī text. The teaching closely resembles that of Edict XI., which treats of True Piety. The word *maṅgalam* rendered by 'ceremonial' or 'ceremonies' is specially applied in the Jātakas to the worship of the Hindu deities, and includes all rites intended to win the favour of unseen powers.

Sickness.—So Kern and Senart. Others render 'misfortunes' or 'trouble.'

ROCK EDICT X.

The variations in the texts do not seriously affect the sense, which is certain. The Girnār text has been translated. The subject matter is closely connected with that of Edict XIII., which deals with True Conquest. The necessity for strenuous exertion, further enforced in the Minor Rock Edicts, is a favourite topic of the Buddhist scriptures, as, for instance, the saying in the *Dhammapada*, 'Diligence is the way to deliverance, sloth is the way to spiritual death.'

Vice (*apuṇyaṃ*).—The contrary of what is meritorious and virtuous (*puṇyaṃ*).

High degree.—Compare 'It is hard for a rich man to enter into the kingdom of heaven' (*Matt.*, XIX., 23).

Difficult.—'Exceedingly difficult' in Dhauli text.

ROCK EDICT XI.

The translation is from the Shāhbāzgarhi text; the other texts exhibiting slight variations. The language of previous edicts, especially III. and IX., is here applied to a distinct subject matter. The neatest commentary is supplied by Oliver Cromwell's earliest extant letter (dated St. Ives, 11 January, 1635):—'Building of hospitals provides for men's bodies; to build material temples is judged a work of piety; but they that procure spiritual food, they that build up spiritual temples, they are the men truly charitable, truly pious.' We may also compare with advantage the account of Niśśanka Malla, King of Ceylon (1187-96 A.D.) given in an inscription on a rock near one of the alms-houses (*dāna sālā*) erected by him, which runs as follows :—'This pious monarch enjoyed the bliss of almsgiving, as he sat, granting largess with great happiness, hearing many joyous shouts of "*sādhu*" and the like, and imparting the gift of piety (*dāna dharma*) which is the noblest of all gifts.'

Virtue (*puṇyaṃ*)—contrasted with *apuṇyaṃ* of Edict X. The word translated 'meritorious' is *sādhu* (Bühler), but it might be rendered as 'right,' 'proper' or 'excellent.' M. Senart has '*ce qui est bien*.'

ROCK EDICT XII.

Although the language of this curious edict is involved, the interpretation is nearly free from uncertainty. The word *pāsaṃḍa* is best rendered by 'denomination,' as in Rock Edict VII., which should be compared, but the shorter word 'sect' is used here for convenience, because it is so often repeated. Asoka held that all the Indian religions of his time—Buddhism, Jainism, and Hinduism in their various forms—had much in common, and that a preference for one should not blind a man to the merits of the others. In Pillar Edict VI. he repeats the declaration of his reverence for all religious communities, while insisting at the same time that every man should be devoted to his own particular creed. Miss Noble has grasped Asoka's idea and expressed it well in the following passages :—'It is natural enough to the Hindu intellect that around each such forth-shining of the Divine should grow up a new religious system or Church. But each of these is only a special way of expressing the one fundamental doctrine of Māyā, a new mode of endearing God to man. At the same time it is thought that everyone, while recognizing the perfect sympathy of various faiths for one another, should know how to choose one among them for his own, and persist in it, till by its means he has reached a point where the formulæ of sects are meaningless to him. . . . "A man has a right to hold his own belief, but never to force it upon another," is the dictum that has made of India a perfect university of religious culture, including every phase and stage of thought and practice' (*The Web of Indian Life*, pp. 224, 281).

Similarly the author of the *Bhakta-Kalpadrūma* writes :—'Let every man, so far as in him lieth, help the reading of the scriptures, whether those of his own church or those of another.'

Asoka's policy towards the various religions of his empire is further explained in plainer language in Pillar Edict VII.

I have followed Senart in interpreting *lahukā* and *bahukā* as contrasted substantives meaning respectively 'depreciation' and 'respect.' The interpretation of the term *vrachabhumika* as 'Inspectors,' or possibly, 'night guards,' is conjectural.

Concord—(Girnār); 'self-control' (Shāhbāzgarhi).

Official bodies.—The word is *nikāyā*. Senart renders it by '*corps d' agents*.'

Censors of the women.—The terms used are varied in the different texts. These officials are mentioned specifically only in this edict, but seem to be included among the 'many other high officers' of section 7 of Pillar Edict VII. Their duties probably included a general supervision of female morals as well as the control of the courtezans.

ROCK EDICT XIII.

This celebrated edict, translated from the Shāhbāzgarhi text, is in many respects the most important of Asoka's inscriptions. Its meaning is now fully ascertained, subject to slight doubts concerning a few phrases. It explains definitely the Emperor's devotion to *dharma* as the immediate result of the remorse awakened in him by the horrors of the Kalinga war. Assuming 269 B.C. as the date of his consecration or coronation, the war must be placed in 261-260 B.C., and the beginning of Asoka's life-long devotion to *dharma* may be assigned to the year 260 B.C. The Kalinga Edicts explain the principles followed by the government in the newly annexed province. The kingdom of Kalinga, also called 'the Kalingas,' or 'the three Kalingas,' extended along the coast of Orissa, probably from the Mahānadī on the north to the Godāvarī on the south. So far as appears, no other aggressive war was waged by Asoka during his long reign, but it is, of course, possible that he may have done some fighting during his early unrecorded years.

The sentiment that 'even should anyone do him wrong, it must be borne with by His Sacred Majesty, if it can possibly be borne with' is especially noteworthy. It is again expressed in the Kalinga Borderers' Edict, which took the place in that province of this document. The warning to the forest tribes should be compared with the instructions given to the officials of Kalinga in the Borderers' Edict. The translation of the passage is in accordance with M. Senart's view (*J.R.A.S.*, 1900, p. 339), as modified by Mr. Thomas.

Joyousness.—'The fourth point is the joyousness of the Arhat [Buddhist saint], springing more especially from the emancipation of heart to which he has attained, on which so much stress is laid' (Rhys Davids, *American Lectures*, p. 183). Such laying stress on joyousness is a note of Buddhist, not of Brahmanical, teaching.

Chiefest conquest.—Compare a passage from the *Anguttara Nikāya*: '"Warriors, warriors, Lord, we call ourselves. In what way then are we warriors?" "We wage war, O disciples; therefore are we called warriors."

"Wherefore, Lord, do we wage war?"

"For lofty virtue, for high endeavour, for sublime wisdom; therefore are we called warriors."'

Greek (Yona) king named Antiochus.—Yona or Yavana=Ionian, but the term is used vaguely in Indian literature to indicate the foreign populations beyond the north-western frontiers of India, the Yonas mentioned below. In Asoka's time the Yonas included persons of Greek or Macedonian descent. The Antiochus referred to was Antiochus Theos (acc. about 261 B.C.), the grandson of Seleucus Nicator. 'North of that Antiochus' may be translated 'beyond that Antiochus.' 'The four (4) kings;' the figure 4 is inserted in the text.

Ptolemy, etc.—Ptolemy Philadelphus of Egypt (285-247 B.C.); Antigonus Gonatas, King of Macedonia (278 or 277-239 B.C.); Magas, King of Cyrene to the west of Egypt, and half-brother of Ptolemy Philadelphus (died 258 B.C.); Alexander, King of Epirus, opponent of Antigonus Gonatas (272-? 258 B.C.). The dates of these Kings fix the date of the Edicts and the chronology of Asoka's reign within narrow limits. The same Kings are alluded to in Rock Edict II., as neighbours of Antiochus.

Choḷas, Pāṇḍyas, Ceylon.—See commentary on Rock Edict II.

Yonas.—See above.

Kāmbojas.—A Himalayan nation, perhaps Tibetans. *Nābhapaṃtis.*—Not identified.

Bhojas.—Probably the tribe of that name in Ilichpur, Berār.

Pitinikas—Of Paithan on the upper Godāvarī.

Āndhras.—Between the Godāvarī and Kṛishṇā (Kistna) rivers of the Deccan.

Pulindas.—Probably hill-tribes near the Narbadā; the term is used very vaguely in Sanskrit literature.
Envoys.—Compare Rock Edict II. and the Ceylonese accounts of the missionaries sent out during Asoka's reign.
That delight is only a small matter.—A similar phrase occurs in section V. of Pillar Edict VII.
Conquest by arms.—Literally 'by arrows.'
Joy.—See note above on 'joyousness.'

ROCK EDICT XIV.

No reader of the Rock Edicts can fail to recognize the accuracy of this description of them by their author. They are full of repetitions, slightly varied in form, of favourite ideas and phrases. The Kalinga version omits Nos. XI., XII., and XIII. as unsuitable for that province, substituting two edicts specially adapted to its needs, and not found elsewhere. The promise to have much more written is amply fulfilled by the Pillar Edicts and other documents. In translating the final sentence I now follow Senart (*Ind. Ant.*, XIX., 87; *Inscr. de Piyadasi*, I., 316). Most of the inscriptions have been incised with the most scrupulous care, and engravers' blunders rarely occur.
The Kālsī recension is accompanied by a well-drawn outline of a standing elephant, with the label *Gajatame* in the same character as that used in the edicts, between its legs, which is interpreted as meaning 'the superlative elephant.' A similar drawing seems to have been destroyed at Girnār, where the label survives, and is rendered 'This white elephant is in truth the benefactor of the whole world.' At Dhauli in Orissa the massive fore-part of an elephant carved in the rock looks down upon the inscriptions, and the word 'white,' evidently referring to the animal, is appended to Edict VI. M. Senart is right, I think, in regarding all these elephants as specially Buddhist symbols.

KALINGA EDICT I.

The two Kalinga Edicts were published for the benefit of the province of Kalinga, which had been annexed, as explained in Rock Edict XIII., in 261 B.C., the ninth 'regnal year,' reckoned from Asoka's consecration in about 269 B.C., and take the place of Rock Edicts XI.—XIII., which were not published in Kalinga. They exist in two recensions, incised respectively on rocks at Dhauli in the Purī District, Orissa, and Jaugaḍa in the Ganjām District, Madras. The Borderers' Edict at Dhauli is addressed to the Prince and officers of a town named Tosali, presumably near Dhauli, and the Provincials' Edict at the same place is addressed simply to the officers in charge of that town. The address to the Prince indicates that Tosali, like Ujjain and Taxila, which are mentioned at the end of the Provincials' Edict, was the seat of a Viceroyalty administered by a member of the imperial family. Both of the edicts at Jaugaḍa are addressed to the officers of a town named Samāpā, which has not been identified, but no doubt was near the site of the inscription.

At Jaugaḍa both of the Kalinga Edicts are enclosed in a frame with symbols at the corners separating them from the series of Rock Edicts. At Dhauli the Borderers' Edict is enclosed in a frame, while the Provincials' Edict is engraved to the left of the main series. There is no doubt that the Borderers' Edict, No. 2 of Prinsep, was the first of the two to be engraved. Assuming the date of the Rock Edicts to be 256 B.C., and the date of the conquest of Kalinga to be 261 B.C., the Kalinga Edicts may be dated about 256 or 255 B.C.

At Dhauli the forepart of an elephant, standing about four feet high, cut in the rock and well executed, looks down upon the polished surface, 15 feet by 10, on which the inscriptions are engraved, and the word *sveto*, 'white,' appended to Rock Edict VI., evidently refers to the elephant above. The white elephant was a well-known Buddhist symbol, which recurs at Girnār and Kālsī. A photograph of the Dhauli elephant forms the frontispiece to the *Early History of India* (1908).

The two Kalinga Edicts present special difficulties to the translator on account of the frequent abrupt changes from *oratio obliqua* to oratio *directa*. The Jaugaḍa version of the Borderers' Edict being the better preserved has been translated. The Provincials' Edict, on the other hand, is in much better condition at Dhauli than at Jaugaḍa, and has been chosen for translation. Except for the opening address there is little difference between the versions at the two sites.

Both edicts possess exceptional interest as expositions of Asoka's policy, obviously expressed mainly in his own words, the abrupt transitions from *oratio obliqua* to *oratio directa* being made in order to bring in His Majesty's personal appeals to his officers and people.

A few phrases require brief comment.

My views are.—Literally 'I see.'

All men are my children.—This is an echo of the saying—'All beings are my children,' attributed to Buddha in the *Lotus de la bonne Loi*, p. 89, and the *Dharma-saṅgraha*, II., as quoted by Kern, *Buddhism*, p. 61.

'*Local officials*='superintendents in all countries' (Bühler). M. Senart, taking *desaṃ* to mean 'order' and *āyuktike* to mean 'energetic,' renders '*exécuteurs actifs de mes ordres.*'

Tishya days.—See commentary on Pillar Edict V., *post.*

KALINGA EDICT II.

This edict is to a large extent identical with the one preceding. It is addressed specially to the officers in charge of two towns in the newly conquered province of Kalinga, and charges them to see that justice is done and that the townsmen do not suffer imprisonment or ill-usage without due cause. The concluding paragraphs are of general application and intimate that the principles inculcated will be enforced throughout the empire by officers when on circuit. The circuit will take place at intervals of five years in the provinces under the Emperor's more immediate control, but in the distant viceroyalties of Ujjain and Taxila the Princes are directed to send out their officers on circuit with intervals of only three years. The general rules concerning the circuit (*anusaṃyāna*) are given in Rock Edict III.

The orders here, as in the Borderers' Edict, are based on the fundamental principle that the Emperor is the father of his people, and it seems to me that the references in the text to the 'principle,' 'policy,' or 'moral rule' (*nīti*) apply specially to the proposition affirming the relations of parent and child between the Sovereign and his subjects, which was adapted from a saying of Buddha.

The language is somewhat involved, but the interpretation is almost free from doubt. The correct rendering of the passage beginning 'Ill performance' is due to Prof. Otto Franke of Königsberg. 'Ill-usage' seems to be an adequate equivalent for *parikilesaṃ*, M. Senart's 'torture' being a little too strong. Bühler translates 'serious trouble.'

The Dhauli recension, which is that translated, is addressed to the officers at Tosali; the Jaugaḍa one being addressed to those at Samāpā. The variations between the two texts are unimportant.

PILLAR EDICT I.

This document, which serves as a preface or preamble to the set of Pillar Edicts, offers no serious difficulties of interpretation. We shall meet the King's 'Agents' (*lit.* 'men') again in Edict IV. of this series. They may be identified with the *paṭivedakā* of Rock Edict VI. and the *episkopoi*, of Megasthenes. The edict proclaims that the whole system of government is based upon the principles of *dharma* in the special sense frequently defined, with variations, by the royal author. The proclamation seems to be simply intended for general information, and not to be addressed particularly to officials or any one class of his subjects. The 'self-examination' here alluded to is the special subject of Pillar Edict III.

Fickle minded—chapalaṃ, equivalent to 'sinners' (Bühler). Compare *Arthaśāstra*, Bk. II., ch. 9:—'For men are naturally fickle-minded, and like horses in their work exhibit constant change in their temper.'

PILLAR EDICT II.

This edict offers one more of the many variant definitions of *dharma* which occur in Asoka's inscriptions. *Dharma*, 'piety,' or 'right conduct,' is contrasted with *āsinave*, which is more expressly treated of in the next edict. Scholars differ concerning the derivation and precise meaning of this word *āsinave*, but it is certainly used here in the sense of 'the opposite to *dharma*,' and so may be rendered 'impiety.' In rendering *chakhudāne* as 'the gift of spiritual insight' (*lit.*, 'eye') Bühler's interpretation is followed, as against that of M. Senart. 'The boon of life' also is Bühler's version, and it seems to me to be undoubtedly correct. The phrase 'many good deeds have I done' is repeated from Rock Edict V., and recurs in section 8 of Pillar Edict VII., where His Majesty declares that his good example has been freely imitated.

PILLAR EDICT III.

This edict is closely connected with the one immediately preceding. Both exhortations warn men against *āsinave*, or 'impiety,' here defined as being produced by brutality, cruelty, anger, pride, and jealousy. Although the language of the original is elliptical, and connecting words have to be supplied in translation, the general sense is sufficiently plain. Bühler has been followed in connecting the word 'jealousy' with the preceding enumeration of evil passions. M. Senart construes it with the following sentence and renders, '*Je ne céderai pas à l' envie et je ne calomnierai pas.*' For the rest, the two scholars named are in substantial agreement.

Sees his ill deed.—In literature *pāpa deśanā*='confession of sin;' so here 'sees'='confesses.'

PILLAR EDICT IV.

The interpretation of this interesting edict offers difficulties, to the solution of which several scholars have contributed. The year referred to, the twenty-seventh of the reign reckoning from the consecration, also saw the issue of the stringent code concerning the treatment of animals embodied in the next following document.

The officials called *Rājūkas*, appointed to rule over hundreds of thousands of people, may be regarded as more or less equivalent in rank to modern Commissioners of Divisions, and I therefore translate the term by the word 'Commissioners.' The Rājūkas were superior to the Prādesikas, or District Officers, but were to some extent under the eye of the King's 'Agents' (*lit.* 'men'), who probably should be identified with the *Paṭivedakas*, or 'reporters' of Rock Edict VI., the *episkopoi* of Megasthenes. Asoka announces that he grants to the Commissioners final jurisdiction, free from appeal to other authorities, in order that they may exercise their functions with confidence, feeling assured that nobody could upset their orders, except His Majesty himself. The people are confided to these high officers just as a child is made over to the care of a skilful nurse, whose judgment is not to be questioned. The jurisdiction of the Commissioners, of course, extended to capital cases. With the object of ensuring uniformity of procedure, Asoka lays down the rule that the condemned prisoners in the provincial jails must invariably be allowed an interval of three days between sentence and execution, and expresses the hope that the interval will be used by the condemned men in meditations suitable to their position, and by their relatives in acts of piety. In this way he trusts that the convicts may gain heaven, while pious practices will be promoted among the general public. Interpreted thus all the parts of the edict have a logical connexion. The terms of the order show that Asoka, like other Buddhist Kings, had no compunction in shedding the blood of responsible human beings, although extremely careful to preserve the lives of even the most insignificant animals, which are not responsible for their acts. It is hardly necessary to observe that the usual practice under the despotic governments of India was for execution to follow instantly upon sentence, and that the grant of even three days' respite was an innovation on established custom.

Through the (subordinate) officials of the Law of Piety.—I now think, with Mr. F. W. Thomas, that this must be the meaning of *dhaṃmayutena*, and not 'in accordance with the principles of the sacred law,' as Bühler, or, 'together with the faithful,' as Senart. Compare *yutā*='officials' in Rock Edict III. and the frequent use of the word in that sense in the *Arthaśāstra*. The Agents were expected to convey exhortations through subordinates as a rule but were recommended to preach personally in certain cases (*kāni*). In Rock Edict V. also it is better to render *dhaṃmayutasa* and *dhaṃmayutānaṃ* as 'subordinate officials of the Law' than as 'the lieges.' So in Pillar Edict VII., section 3, the *dhaṃma-mahāmāta* are required to teach their subordinate *janaṃ dhaṃma-yutaṃ*.

In security and quietness='confidently and quietly' (Michelson).

PILLAR EDICT V.

The purport of this remarkable edict is fully intelligible, but some of the animals named cannot be identified at present, and the rules concerning certain days require explanation.

Parrots.—Presumably the common green parrot.

Starlings.—The familiar Indian *maina*, *Acridotheres tristis.*

(?) *Adjutants.*—A conjectural rendering of *alune*.

'*Brahmani ducks*,'—or 'ruddy geese,' the *chakravāka* of Sanskrit poetry, *chakwa-chakwī* in Hindī, the commonplace example of conjugal fidelity.

Geese (*haṃse*).—Probably including various species, perhaps swans among them. Figures of geese appear on some of Asoka's pillars.

Nandī-mukhas, gelātas.—Unidentified birds.

Bats.—Used by Pāsīs and such low-caste folk in Bengal as food. The people of Coorg consider the flesh of bats to be very strengthening diet. Bühler's proposal to render by 'flying-foxes' seems to be erroneous.

Queen-ants.—Much esteemed as an aphrodisiac.

Female tortoises (*duḍi*).—This rendering seems to be more correct than

Bühler's 'terrapins.' The terrapin is a small tortoise often found in Indian gardens. Tortoises are said to be considered sacred by Buddhists in China.

'*Boneless fish.*'—Not identified, possibly 'prawns.' The 'boneless fish' of Hesiod is interpreted as 'cuttle-fish.'

Vedaveyakas.—Possibly 'eels.'

Gangāpuṭakas.—some river animal (? porpoises).

(?) *Skate.*—A fish that contracts itself.

Tortoises.—Perhaps the river kind.

Porcupines.—One of the five or six 'five-toed' animals allowed by the ancient authorities to be lawful food, but subsequently forbidden.

Bārasingha stags.—Bühler's guess.

'*Brāhmani bulls.*'—The dedicated animals let loose to roam at will, and often a great nuisance. Trouble arises nowadays when, as sometimes happens, a Musalman kills one.

(?) *Monkeys* (*okapiṇḍas*).—The *ukkapiṇḍaka* is described in a Buddhist book as stealing the monks' provisions, which monkeys are prone to do.

Rhinoceros.—Comes in oddly here, but the reading is certain. Ancient authorities permitted the flesh to be eaten.

Grey doves.—Very common in Northern India.

Village pigeons.—The 'blue-rock' common about village wells.

All four-footed animals, etc.—That is to say, no animal must be killed which is not needed for the use of man. This rule has the effect of prohibiting 'sport' as such.

Chaff—is sometimes burned in order to destroy vermin.

The living, etc.—As hawks with the blood of living pigeons, a cruel practice still sometimes followed.

Forests, etc.—Burma offers an illustration. 'During the progress of the first rise [of the river] some hunters went to one of these islands where many deer were to be found, and set fire to the grass to drive them out of cover, shooting them as they came out' (*The Soul of a People*, p. 299). Of course, such conduct is abominable in the eyes of respectable Burmese Buddhists, who regard hunters with loathing and contempt.

Elephant-preserves.—Elephant catching always has been, and still is a State monopoly.

Fish-ponds.—A free rendering of the compound meaning 'place used by fishermen.'

Castration.—Previous to the Muhammadan conquest the Hindus of Bengal are said to have considered the practice to be 'very illegal and disgraceful, not fit to be mentioned' (*E. India*, II., 891). I-tsing (Takakusu, p. 197) says that 'the Buddha did not even allow castration.' Asoka regulates it, but does not prohibit it, except in the case of cocks, which are mutilated merely to improve their flavour as food.

Branding.—In ancient Ceylon the marks used to indicate the caste, village, or family of the owner as well as his name (*Ceylon Nat. Rev.*, Jan., 1907, p. 334). The word rendered 'oxen' here is the same which is rendered 'bulls' above.

Tishya, etc.—In ancient India, as still in rural places, the year was divided into three seasons of four months each, hot, rainy and cold. The reckoning probably used by Asoka made the year begin with the month Chaitra (March—April), each month and season ending with a full-moon day. Tishya and Punarvasu are lucky constellations in which the moon is supposed to be on certain days. Four *uposatha*, 'fast' or 'sabbath' days, fell in each month, viz., the 8th and either the 14th or 15th day of each fortnight; on which days people were expected to fast and suspend all business, as is now done in Burma. The rules laid down by Asoka give fish a close time of 56 days in all. Castration and branding are treated by him as unholy, although necessary acts, not to be performed on days regarded as holy for any reason.

Minute regulations such as those published in this edict must have given rise to much espionage and vexatious tyranny by petty officials. No doubt the enforcement of such rules was the principal business of the *Dharmamahāmātras*, or Censors of the Law of Piety, and their subordinates, the *Dharmayuktas*. If we may judge from the recorded action of certain Hindu rulers in later ages, breach of the rules must have been visited by severe penalties, extending even to the infliction of death on the offender.

The last sentence of the edict dealing with jail deliveries or the release of prisoners apparently must be understood as referring only to prisoners condemned to death, whose case alone would be relevant to the general tenor of the document. The wretches who benefited by the royal clemency on the coronation day cannot have been numerous, because Edict IV. above proves that the grant of even three days' respite between sentence and execution was an innovation on established practice. Chāṇakya lays down the rule that prisoners should be released on the occasions of annexation of a country by conquest, the installation or consecration of the Rājā, or the birth of a prince (*Ind. Ant.*, XXXIV., 52).

PILLAR EDICT VI.

This document does not present much difficulty. The reference to 'pious edicts' (*dhaṃmalipi*) obviously applies particularly to Rock Edicts III. and IV. which are dated in the thirteenth year of the reign. M. Senart, no doubt, is right in holding that Asoka means that his earliest edicts date from that year. The Minor Rock Edicts of Sahasrām, etc., apparently belong to nearly the same time. The phrase 'giving up their old courses' is a slight amplification of the laconic text, 'giving up that' (*tam apahaṭa*) as interpreted by Bühler. Senart renders 'picking up something (of the teaching).' 'One way or another' expresses the distributive force of *taṃ taṃ*. The phrase about reverence to all denominations is taken from Rock Edict XII. The vague word 'communities' seems to be the best rendering of *nikāya*, which has more meanings than one. 'Adherence to one's own creed,' Senart's interpretation, is preferable to that of Bühler, who understood the King to allude to 'the voluntary approach which one sect is to make towards the other,' as advised in Rock Edict XII.

PILLAR EDICT VII.

The language of this edict—much the longest in the collection—is characterized by frequent repetitions, such as are mentioned in the Epilogue to the Fourteen Rock Edicts. These redundancies of expression have been slightly pruned in the translation. The purpose of the document is to pass in review the measures taken by Asoka during his reign to promote the knowledge and practice of *dharma*, the Law of Piety, or whole duty of man, as interpreted in a Buddhist sense. The composition may be regarded as comprising ten separate edicts, each beginning with the phrase 'Thus saith His Majesty,' slightly varied. Of these ten edicts or sections, No. I. is merely a brief preamble reciting the failure of former Kings to secure the desired development of piety, or *dharma*. The beginning of Rock Edict IV. may be compared.

No. II. repeats the preamble and records how Asoka reflected on the means required to obtain better results.

In No. III. His Majesty expounds his arrangements for preaching the Law of Piety as carried out under the supervision of the Commissioners (*Rājūkas*), mentioned in Rock Edict III.

No. IV. enumerates three other measures taken to effect the royal purpose, namely, the erection of pillars inscribed with the teachings of the Law, the appointment of Censors (*dharmamahāmātrā*), and the composition of precepts, or rather, a precept of the Law. The saying quoted in the First Minor Rock Edict, 'Let small and great exert themselves,' appears to be such a precept (*sāvane*) composed (*kaṭe*) by Asoka. The last sentence of Rock Edict X. may be another, and several other formulæ in various edicts look as if they were framed by Asoka himself. The appointment of Censors in the fourteenth 'regnal year' is recorded in Rock Edict V.

The works executed for the material comfort of man and beast by the King's command are specified in section No. V. of this document in words partly copied from Rock Edict II. '*At every half-kōs*.' This is the correct translation. It is objected that the intervals are incredibly short, and that we should translate 'at intervals of eight *kōs*,' the ordinary length of a day's march. But the text will hardly bear this construction, and we must remember that, according to Strabo, Chandragupta's 'mile-stones' were set up at intervals of ten *stadia*=$2022\frac{1}{2}$ yards=about half a *kōs*. Perhaps the wells at each mile-stone were only earthen ones.

Section VI. deals with the duties of the Censors, which are described also in Rock Edict V. The two documents when read together show that the Censors were charged with multifarious, delicate duties, and enjoyed extensive powers, but the exact manner in which these officers worked with the departmental officials is not explained.

The subject of section VII. is what may be called the Royal Almoner's Department, administered by the Censors and other officers of high degree. The short Queen's Edict, inscribed on the Allahabad pillar as a supplement to the set of Pillar Edicts, was issued in that department. The Queens were the ladies bearing the official title of *Devī*, and the princes (*devīkumara*) were their sons. The other sons of the King referred to may be understood as meaning his offspring by concubines or consorts of rank inferior to the Queens. The list of virtues recommended agrees nearly, but not exactly, with that given in Pillar Edict II.

In section VIII. the royal author proceeds to speak of his own meritorious deeds, and the good example set by him, as expounded in Pillar Edict II. The catalogue of meritorious deeds may be compared with the similar lists in Rock Edicts III., IV., V., IX., XI., and XIII., and the Second Minor Rock Edict.

Section IX. classifies the means for the increase of the practice of *dharma* under two heads, namely, formal regulations and meditation, the latter being pronounced to be much the more valuable. Special allusion is made to the detailed regulations embodied in Pillar Edict V. The phrase 'so long as the sun and moon endure' recurs in the Cave Dedications. The section closes with the date, the 28th 'regnal year' (269-27=242 B.C.).

The final section, No. X., consists of a brief command to inscribe the edict on pillars and tables of stone, wheresoever they may exist. This command does not seem to have been carried out. Copies of the first six Pillar Edicts, inscribed on six monuments (Delhi—Topra; Delhi—Meerut; Allahabad—Kauśāmbī; Lauṛiyā—Araṛāj; Lauṛiyā—Nandangaṛh; and Rāmpurwā), are known, but Edict VII., the most important of all, is found on the first-named only. No rock-cut copy of any of the Pillar Edicts has yet been discovered.

MINOR PILLAR EDICT I.

This interesting edict, inscribed on a fallen column, once crowned by a magnificent lion capital, was discovered at Sārnāth near Benares by Mr. F. O. Oertel in 1905. The first three lines are badly damaged, but the rest, the essential part of the document, is practically perfect. The inscription has been studied by Messrs. Boyer, Senart, Thomas, Vogel, and Venis, and its meaning is now well ascertained, subject to slight differences of opinion concerning certain minute details.

It seems that the ordinance must have been addressed to the officials generally, both those at the capital, Pāṭaliputra, and in the provinces, but unfortunately the injury to the first three lines is so great that the opening sentence cannot be restored. The first intelligible proposition is the definite statement that no person is at liberty to rend in twain the *Saṃgha*, that is, to cause schism in the Buddhist Church, the monastic organization of monks and nuns. The edict then goes on to prescribe the penalty to be inflicted on a schismatic person, namely expulsion or suspension from the Order and exclusion from places appropriated for monastic residence. The expulsion or suspension was to be signified by divesting the offender of his orange-coloured monastic robe and clothing him in white garments as worn by the laity, in short, 'unfrocking' him. The same penalty for schism is mentioned by Buddhaghosa in his account of the Council convened by Asoka at Pāṭaliputra. Similar orders are given in the Sānchī Pillar Edict, and the Kauśāmbī Edict on the Allahabad pillar.

The rest of the document is devoted to rules concerning the publication of the royal orders, which were to be communicated to all congregations (*saṃgha*) of monks and nuns, as well as the laity. The officials are reminded that one copy has been posted up (? 'inscribed') in their (?) head office (*saṃsaraṇa*), and are commanded to send out copies textually correct throughout all parts of their immediate jurisdictions, and to communicate other equally accurate to the governors of garrisons and districts.

The word used for District (*visava=vishaya*) signified in later times the area now known as a *pargana*, and may have had the same meaning in Asoka's days. Each *vishaya* was under the administration of a *vishayapati*. So each garrison or fortified place (*koṭa*) was commanded by a governor. The double causal form of the verb indicates that in such garrisons and Districts the royal orders were to be communicated through the responsible local officials. M. Boyer, accordingly, translates the verb *vivāsayātha* by *faites partir*, *envoyez*,' and *vivāsāpayātha* by *faites envoyer*.'

The meaning of *koṭa* is illustrated by the rules in Chāṇakya's treatise on Polity, which prescribe that 'The King shall open out new villages, consisting of from a hundred to five hundred houses. . . . A fortress of wooden posts shall be constructed round every village at a distance of a hundred yards from it. . . . The centre of eight hundred villages shall be the seat of a fortress called *Sṭhānīya*, etc.' (*Ind. Ant.*, XXXIV., 7).

This edict is of much interest to the historian of Buddhism as proving the early completeness of the monastic organization under the supreme control of the King as Head of the Church, and confirming the literary tradition that Asoka dealt sternly with schismatic heretics. It contains no explicit indication of date. The conjecture of one author assigns it to the year (about 249 B.C.) when Asoka made a pilgrimage to the holy places, including Sārnāth. If this conjecture were correct, the edict would be approximately contemporary with the Tarāi Pillar Inscriptions. But the substantially identical ordinance in the Kauśāmbi Edict on the Allahabad pillar clearly is later in date than the six Pillar Edicts of the 27th 'regnal year' (243 B.C.) on that monument, and the Sārnāth document, as well as the similar one at Sānchī, probably should be assigned to the same period. It seems reasonable to suppose that the orders in these documents resulted from the deliberations of the Council of Pāṭaliputra vouched for by literary tradition. On this supposition the date of the Council will fall between 243 and 232, the date of Asoka's death.

MINOR PILLAR EDICT II.

This brief and much mutilated edict was discovered by Cunningham on the Allahabad pillar, which bears a copy of the first six Pillar Edicts, and many inscriptions of later date. The long inscription of Samudragupta (about 380 A.D.) comes immediately below the six Pillar Edicts, and its upper portion is confined between a crack in the stone on the left and two short Asoka inscriptions on the right. The lower one of those two is the Queen's Edict, the upper one, in four lines, largely obliterated by later records, is the order to the officials of Kauśāmbī translated above so far as is possible. The ordinance prescribing the unfrocking and expulsion of schismatic persons from the Buddhist Church or Order (*saṃgha*) is the same as that incised on the Sānchī and Sārnāth pillars.

The existence of this edict on the Allahabad pillar affords almost conclusive evidence that that monument was removed from Kauśāmbī. Cunningham's conjecture that the removal was effected in the fourteenth century by Fīrōz Tughlak is highly probable. The site of the *Buddhist* Kauśāmbī or Kosambi has not yet been determined. In my opinion it lay about ninety miles from Allahabad in a south-westerly direction. Kosam on the Jumna about thirty miles above Allahabad is a Jain site, and is recognized as the ancient Kauśambī by the Jains, but the Kauśāmbī of the Buddhist records was another place.

MINOR PILLAR EDICT III.

This mutilated document is incised on a broken pillar near the great *stūpa* at Sānchī in the Bhopāl State, Central India. The pillar, like that at Sārnāth, was once crowned by a fine lion capital. M. Boyer's attempt to fill up the lacuna after the word 'made' is too conjectural to justify translation. The command is the same as that recorded in the Sārnāth and Kauśāmbī Edicts. The concluding sentence expressing the royal desire that 'the Way of the Church may long endure' may be compared with the Kauśāmbī precept that 'the Way of the Church must not be quitted.' The earlier interpreters erroneously supposed this inscription to allude to a material road or procession path.

MINOR PILLAR EDICT IV.

This brief edict, incised on the Allahabad pillar below the Kauśāmbi Edict, evidently was, like that document, an addition to the record made after the inscription of the six Pillar Edicts had been finished. Both of the short edicts, therefore, must be not earlier in date than the 27th 'regnal year' (243 B.C.). The order is one made in the Royal Almoner's Department mentioned in section VII. of Pillar Edict VII. It throws a welcome ray of light on the personal history of Asoka by proving that in the latter part of his reign he had at least two consorts with the official title of Queen (*devī*), the second of whom was known by her family name as 'the Kāruvāki,' and was the mother of a prince named Tīvara. His fate is not recorded, but he did not succeed his father, who seems to have been followed directly by his grandson Daśaratha, whose dedicatory inscriptions exist in the Nāgārjuni caves. With the exception of a few words the Queen's Edict is perfectly preserved. The small gap has been filled conjecturally. The lettering is more roughly executed than that of the other inscriptions.

TARĀI PILLAR INSCRIPTION I.

The pillar stands at a shrine called Rummindēī in the Nepalese Tarāi, not far from the village of Paḍaria and a few miles from the north-eastern corner of the British district of Bastī. Rummin-dēī is the Luṃmini of the record, and there is no doubt that the monument occupies its original position and marks the site of the Lumbini Garden, the traditional scene of the birth of Gautama, the Buddha, the sage of the Sakya or Sākya clan, which had its headquarters at Kapilavastu a few miles distant.

The inscription is absolutely perfect (see facsimile in *Asoka, the Buddhist Emperor of India*, plate II.) and every letter is legible with certainty. The difficulties of interpretation are chiefly concerned with the two compound words *silāvigaḍabhīchā* and *aṭhabhāgiye*, which are peculiar to this document. Various attempts have been made to explain these words and the version above gives what now seems to me to be the most probable rendering.

Whatever may be the exact meaning of the disputed words there is no doubt that the costly pillar was erected by Asoka to commemorate his visit to one of the four holiest shrines of Buddhism, when he was engaged on a 'pious tour' such as is described in Rock Edict VIII. The memory of this particular tour in the twenty-first 'regnal year' (about 249 B.C.) is preserved by the *Asokāvadāna* romance, which relates that Asoka first visited the Lumbini Garden under the guidance of his teacher Upagupta, who made use of the very words incised on the pillar, 'Here the Venerable One was born.' (Burnouf, *Introduction*, 2nd ed., p. 341). The form of the inscription suggests that Asoka intended to quote his *guru's* words.

In interpreting *mahīyite* as 'did reverence' I follow the competent authority of the late Professor Pischel and other eminent scholars. Dr. Fleet's rival interpretation is based on a theory of Asoka's conversion to Buddhism late in his reign which seems to me to be wholly erroneous.

Free of religious cesses, etc.—The best possible commentary on the technical legal terms *ubalikekaṭe aṭhabhāgiyecha* is a quotation from Chāṇakya's *Arthaśāstra*, Bk. II., ch. 15:—'Taxes that are fixed [i.e. on whole villages, *Comm.*], *pindakara*; taxes that are paid in the form of one-sixth of produce [including 'one-fourth,' 'one-third,' etc., *Comm.*], *shaḍbhāga*, etc.' In short, the two terms mean 'exempt from paying revenue and cesses,' in the language of a modern 'Settlement Officer.'

TARAI PILLAR II.

This broken pillar is lying by the side of a lake about thirteen miles to the north-west of Rummindēī and near the site of Hiuen Tsang's Kapilavastu, now Tilaurā Kōṭ. It does not occupy its original position, but does not seem to have been moved any great distance. Although the inscription is damaged, the first date is legible, and the second may be filled in with confidence by comparison with the similar record at Rummindēī.

Buddhists believed that Gautama Buddha, the Sakya sage, had been preceded by a long series of 'former Buddhas,' among whom only the last three, namely, Krakuchanda or Kakusanda, Kanakamuni or Konākamana, and Kāśyapa or Kassapa, have any claim to historical reality. This record proves that as early as 255 B.C. Asoka had enlarged for the second time the *stūpa* of Konākamana, and that six years later he marched from Rummindēī and paid the *stūpa* a personal vist. Very little is known about the 'former Buddhas,' and it is extremely interesting to learn that Asoka paid honour to them as well as to their great successor, his revered Master. The enlargement of the *stūpa* is readily understood when we remember that many examples are known of the addition of outer casings to ancient *stūpas*; indeed, every important monument of the class has been the subject of frequent rebuilding.

Some years ago when in the Tarāi I heard various stories of the existence of other pillars in that region and am convinced that they exist, but it is not easy to find them in Nepalese territory. Probably a long series of pillars marked the line of Asoka's 'pious tour.' I believe that many more inscriptions of Asoka remain to be discovered.

The three pillars in the Champāran District which bear copies of the first six Pillar Edicts have nothing to do with the 'pious tour,' but mark the line of the high road from the capital to the valley of Nepāl, and were so placed that travellers might learn the Law of Piety. The inscriptions on the two Tarāi pillars are the only commemorative records of Asoka as yet disclosed.

THE BARĀBAR CAVE DEDICATIONS.

The Barābar Hills stand fifteen or sixteen miles in a direct line, or nineteen by road, to the north of Gayā. Four caves have been excavated with infinite labour in remarkably shaped masses of quartzose gneiss. One of these caves, now known by the name of Lomas Rishi, is unfinished and has no inscription. The other three were dedicated by Asoka, two when he had been consecrated twelve years, and the third seven years later.

The inscription in the third cave is so much damaged that it is impossible to say to whom the dwelling was granted. The first two caves were bestowed on the Ājīvikas, who are mentioned in Pillar Edict VII. along with Jains and Buddhists as one of the leading sects or denominations of the time. They were naked ascetics, addicted to rigorous pennance, and, as Professor Bhandarkar has shown, closely related to the Jains. By granting them costly benefactions Asoka proved the sincerity of his declarations that he did reverence to all denominations. Buddhist literature shows that the Ājīvikas were regarded with intense aversion by many Buddhists.

The simple royal title 'Rājā Piyadasi' is best translated by the old Tudor phrase the 'King's Grace.' The earlier date, it will be observed, is the same as that of Rock Edicts III. and IV., equivalent to about 257 B.C. Pillar Edict VI. proves that Asoka began his practice of recording imperishable inscriptions in that year. The second date (250 B.C.) precedes by a year the imperial visit to the birth-place of Buddha. The phrase 'as long as sun and moon endure' recurs in Pillar Edict VII. and in the dedications of Daśaratha.

The cost of these cave-dwellings must have been enormous, the excavations being of considerable size and the internal walls and roofs being for the most part highly polished. The stone is of the hardest and most refractory character. Without going into wearisome detail, it will suffice to state that the Sudāma cave is a vaulted chamber 33 feet long, 19 feet broad, and 12½ feet high, with every inch of the walls and roof burnished like glass. There is also an interior domed recess or chapel, unfinished.

THE NĀGĀRJUNI CAVE DEDICATIONS.

The three caves in the Nāgārjuni hills are about a mile distant from the Barābar caves, and were dedicated by Daśaratha, who is recorded in the Purāṇas to have been Asoka's grandson. The wording of the dedications is remarkable in that the title 'His Sacred Majesty' (*devānaṃ piyena*) follows the King's name instead of preceding it as usual. This peculiarity has suggested the alternative translation 'assigned by Daśaratha immediately after his consecration by His Sacred Majesty (*scil.* Asoka),' and the words would seem to bear that construction. The Purāṇas represent Daśaratha as the son of Suyaśas, a son of Asoka who reigned for eight years, but the truth may be that Daśaratha succeeded his grandfather immediately. The script of Daśaratha's inscriptions does not differ from that of Asoka's.

The Gopikā cave was a most costly work, being 46 feet 5 inches in length by 19 feet 2 inches in breadth, vaulted to a height of 10½ feet with circular ends. The whole of the interior, which is quite plain, has been highly polished. The Barābar and Nāgārjuni hills still are inhabited by ascetics and visited by pilgrims. The whole locality has a strangely weird and desolate aspect. Indications of old buildings, however, exist, and Cunningham believed that a town once stood within the Barābar ring of hills, but I doubt it.

Printed at the Essex House Press in the Norman Chapel at Broad Campden. Sold at the Essex House Press and by Henry Frowde, Amen Corner, London, E.C.
One hundred copies on hand-made paper, of which this is No. 88.
Finished the 19th day of February, 1909.